IT'S NOT MAGIC

IT'S NOT MAGIC

THE REBIRTH OF A SMALL MANUFACTURING COMPANY

Donald J. Klein
Jim Zawacki

Michigan State University Press
East Lansing

∞ The paper used in this publication meets the minimum requirements of
ANSI/NISO Z39.48-1992 (R 1997) (Permanence of Paper).

Michigan State University Press
East Lansing, Michigan 48823-5202

04 03 02 01 00 99   1 2 3 4 5 6

Library of Congress Cataloging-in-Publication Data

Klein, Don, 1936-
  It's not magic: the rebirth of a small manufacturing company / Don Klein, Jim
Zawacki.
    p. cm.
  ISBN 0-87013-500-7 (alk. paper)
  I. Zawacki, Jim.

PS3561.L3443187 1999   98-043906
813/.54 21   CIP

Cover design by Heidi Dailey.
Book design by Michael J. Brooks.

_____

Visit Michigan State University Press on the World-Wide Web at:
    http://www.msu.edu/unit/msupress

Contents

Preface

Think about IBM in 1990. In the previous decade its profits had averaged between eight and nine billion dollars per year. To put this in context in 1997, the two most profitable firms in America, Exxon and GE, each made about 8 billion dollars in profits. Seventeen years earlier IBM was making this amount of money. In 1990 IBM was to make between 10 and 11 billion dollars in profits. Before or after, no other firm has ever made this sum of money. IBM was the most profitable and the most admired firm in human history.

Then God came to John Ackers much as he did to Moses and said, "John come up the mountain with me. I want to show you the promised land. The era of the mainframe computer is over. The PC is here. If you don't adjust to this new reality, profits will fall to zero in 1991, in 1992 you will lose 9 billion dollars, in 1993 this will be repeated, and in 1994 you will lose another 5 billion dollars for a total of 23 billion dollars in losses. No firm before or since has ever lost so much money. It is now your job John to go down the mountain and persuade 420,000 employees who have had the best decade in human history and the best year in human history that they must rip it all up and do something very different."

Could you do that? Could anyone do that? I suspect that God himself could not have managed IBM successfully. It is important to remember that the ten commandments themselves had to be brought down the mountain twice by Moses before they were believed.

Not every firm will fall off a cliff the way IBM did, but every firm is going to go through an IBM experience. Slowly or rapidly the world that brought them into existence is going to go out of existence and they are going to have to become something quite different if they want to survive.

At a very different size level *It's Not Magic* deals with the IBM problem in a small firm where its markets (cables for rear view mirrors) were also becoming obsolete. The advantage of studying a turn-around in a small firm is that it is possible to see what was done and to learn from that turn-around how it might be done in other small firms. Few of us are going to lead and manage multi-billion dollar firms. Many of us are going to have to lead and manage small organizations.

It's Not Magic tells its story in an engaging conversational way, but the bottom line how-to-do-it principles are here.

Focus on the weak links since no chain is better than its weakest link.

Grow people that are willing to make the necessary changes. In the end leadership and management is about persuading people to change.

Quality is not job number one. It is the only job. Without it there is only failure.

Everyone must be a leader to visualize where the organization needs to go and a manager to get it there.

Trust, relationships, integrity, and communications are not the name of the game. They are the game.

Toxic people can be detoxified.

Small steps lead to big revolutions. There are no magic silver bullets.

Suddenly turning the place upside down leads to chaos—not success.

Persistence is the ultimate virtue. Turn-arounds take time!

Between the lines an implicit message twinkles out. Smile! It is more fun solving difficult business and human problems if you do. And you are more likely to succeed.

Lester Thurow

Introduction

This book is the story of a real company, a company that transformed itself from a struggling supplier to a leading small manufacturer of springs and stampings. It used to be similar to many small manufacturing businesses in the United States, and we are convinced that many small manufacturing businesses can become like Magic, Inc.; successful because all the talents and energy of its people are directed together at learning, change, and improvement.

It's Not Magic is really a two-part story. Part of that story, the part in this book, is about the people and personalities involved in the company's transformation. We think it is a triumph by a group of people who faced up to business realities in the current and coming business world. We were part of that group, but credit belongs to more people than we can name. The second part of the story is told by the processes and programs—the tools that allowed us to change Magic, Inc. These tools—the charts and lists, the questions and questionnaires—were important; so important that we wanted to make them available to other companies. We have published these tools in a companion workbook.

The nonfictional story behind *It's Not Magic* began in 1985, when Jim and his partner Ted Hohman purchased GR Spring and Stamping (GRSS). Ted has been a great supporter of all the changes at GRSS. Like many suppliers, GRSS was struggling with new realities. It simply had not faced them. GRSS had no quality systems, no statistical process control (SPC), no computers, no tracking systems, no training program, and no engineers. This was only twelve years ago! Looking back, it is hard to believe that GRSS had survived as long as it had.

The company had to make a change. Don joined the plot in 1987. His academic background and knowledge of current management practices

1

and theories deepened the process of finding a way for GRSS to survive. We have worked together since then, buoyed and heartened by the people at GRSS, who for the most part easily have seen the problems and have thrown themselves into finding solutions.

The results have been astonishing—even to us. Now GRSS has found financial stability and quality improvement that has lowered our costs. We became ISO 9002 registered and QS 9000 compliant in July of 1996. The International Standards Organization set into place worldwide accepted quality standards of measurement for registration. Our on-time deliveries are close to 100 percent. We have 50 computers for our one hundred associates—we have become a technological leader in our field. Our Capability Process Index (CPK) averages 1.75. We implemented twelve improvement ideas per associate in 1996. We have had only one lost-time accident in the last eight years. We have reduced inventory by 30 percent, even though sales have tripled. We have no time clocks and a life-long education program. There are no barriers between the office and the plant. In fact, there are no barriers at all between groups of people at GRSS. Most encouraging and promising of all, we have a culture that shows its commitment daily to continuous improvement. It is hard to believe all that has happened in twelve short years.

Perhaps the most important result of this story was all that we ourselves learned. We have written this book and the companion workbook to pass along to others the things we have learned and the improvements we are sure can take place in other companies. If your company needs to change, if you are convinced that what you are doing now in your business will not be sufficient for you to survive in the coming years—we are certain you will find something of value in the story of Magic, Inc.

1

Peter Thompson Meets Professor John Keen

A Chance to Learn

Driving to his first meeting with Peter Thompson of Magic Manufacturing, Professor John Keen still could not believe his good fortune. He was going to be studying world-class manufacturing techniques and concepts in an actual manufacturing plant. And this magnificent opportunity had all come about as the result of a chance meeting with Peter six days ago.

Keen remembered Peter's first question upon meeting. "What do you do for a living?" To which Keen had replied that he was a teacher at Muscadine University.

"I'm not currently teaching," Keen said. "I have a sabbatical leave from the university this semester, and I'm studying world-class manufacturing concepts."

A spark of interest came to Peter's eyes as he asked the professor how he was doing this.

"I'm attending a number of seminars, reading about it in different books and magazine articles, and visiting companies when I have the opportunity."

Shortly into their conversation, the professor noticed that he and Peter were talking the same language. Then Keen began to see an opportunity starting to take shape. What he would give to see his and others' theories tested in a working, small manufacturing business! He had read plenty about large corporations but not much about smaller ones.

When Peter asked Keen if he was familiar with world-class manufacturing and just-in-time (JIT) techniques, the professor said he was but admitted that he had learned everything from textbooks. He had not had any hands-on experience.

"Would you like to sit in with us at our plant and learn along with us?" Peter asked. "It would be a way for you to get some firsthand experience. We could benefit from the knowledge you've acquired from all your studies."

Keen could not believe it. A chance to learn how the business world does things. Most professors seldom get to see where the rubber meets the road. But here was an opportunity to learn along with workers and managers in a manufacturing plant.

Keen then recalled of the subsequent telephone conversation with Peter two days later. The two men ended up talking for nearly thirty minutes. During the chat, Peter discussed how he had bought Magic Manufacturing eleven months previous. "When I bought the company, it employed about sixty people, sales were $7 million, and one product line—cables for exterior automotive mirrors—represented 50 percent of the sales," Peter said.

"At the time of the purchase, I wasn't aware that the automotive industry was phasing out these cables for exterior mirrors," Peter went on. "The cables were being replaced by electronically controlled mirrors. Within a few months after I bought the company, the phaseout caused our orders to drop dramatically. Over the next twelve months I suspect that the cables will become totally obsolete." Peter paused. "This is a good example of the life cycle of a product. You have to keep up with new technologies and changes. With all of the new technological advances I believe we're going to see things changing at a very rapid pace."

Peter continued. "Besides our most profitable product dropping 70 percent in dollar volume during the past eleven months, and profits in a severe decline because of the product being phased out, we also have other challenges and threats to our survival."

Keen had to know more. When Peter hung up, Keen just sat at his desk with the phone cradled on his shoulder. He hoped that perhaps at today's meeting he would learn about Magic's other problems. His mind began to wander again. He began to think about JIT, total quality management (TQM), employee empowerment, and other voguish issues. Each emphasized changing an organization's culture and involving workers in the decision process. Few articles or books really talked about the specifics. In theory these issues are straightforward, but in reality they do not seem to happen very often. "Is there any magic behind changing culture and how to get people truly involved in making decisions, especially in medium-sized organizations?" the professor mused. "Maybe this is the experiential learning opportunity that I have been looking for. Maybe Peter and I can learn together how to change culture and grow people."

2

First Visit to Magic

"Theory and Practice Have to Be Forged Together if an
Organization Wants to Be Successful" Dr. Deming

In preparation for the day's meeting, Keen reviewed all of his information about world-class manufacturing, JIT, TQM, Theory of Constraints (TOC), empowerment of employees, and other techniques. He was determined to know as much—at least theoretically—as anyone else in the room. And he not only wanted to learn, he also wanted to contribute. But most of what he read concerned large corporations. Could Magic Manufacturing actually put some of these concepts into place—right in his own backyard?

Keen began to think about the future of Magic Manufacturing. He could not help but wonder if the company would survive. The phaseout of the cables was going to wipe out 60 percent of Magic's sales and almost all of its profits. And hadn't Peter said there were more problems? But it seemed that Peter wanted to at least try to turn things around.

Keen's excitement was practically uncontrollable as he pulled into Magic's parking lot. He had not felt this alive in years.

He was greeted in the small lobby by the receptionist, who gave him directions to the meeting. He made his way down the stairs. The session was being held in the largest unoccupied room in the plant, about the size of a large bedroom. As Keen entered the room, he noticed that the lighting was poor and condensation from the many dirty pipes fell everywhere. Along the walls, old plastic shower curtains tried to hide piles of disorganized boxes, parts, records, equipment, and other items from the balance of the small room, used as a learning center. So this was reality.

The professor set his coffee on the wobbly conference table and opened a folding chair with a torn, vinyl-covered, padded seat. He was ready. Peter introduced Keen to the group. They seemed to share Peter's optimism about the future of Magic, though he could sense a tinge of skepticism among them. Besides Keen and Peter, plant manager Fred Ulrich and general manager Chet Franklin sat at the table.

Peter walked around the table and placed a tape into a videocassette recorder. The tape was a fundamental introduction to the basic JIT principles, explaining how plant layouts must be changed, how workers must be educated, that quality control was essential, and that eliminating waste and simplifying everything was imperative. The empowerment of people was necessary.

The ultimate objectives were discussed: minimum inventory, short lead time, zero defects, process flow, flexible manufacturing, and on-time delivery. The tape concluded by citing the major obstacles to a successful JIT program, which were lack of systems support, resistance within the company, no implementation plan, poor quality management, Single Minute Exchange of Die (SMED), a weak preventive maintenance system, and a lack of continuous commitment from management. A commitment from top management was especially important.

Keen remembered seeing this same video a few months ago. Even though he knew most of the information, it somehow seemed different now. Maybe it was the setting. Or maybe it was the other people in the room. After all, it was do-or-die for them.

Everyone watched the video intently. Most took notes. They all agreed that they would like to watch it again at the end of the day. There were no questions and there was very little discussion. The participants were pleasant enough toward Keen, but for the most part they ignored him. They were there for one purpose—to learn how to save their company.

After everyone left, Keen and Peter made small talk and discussed the video. But the professor had some questions nagging at him, and he could not resist asking them. "Last week, you mentioned that there were other problems threatening your company's survival. I'm curious, what are they?"

"Oh, they're no different than the problems at most American companies. But when we found out that we were going to lose such a large amount of our business, I guess I took a more critical look at all of our other operations."

"What did you find?"

Peter was straightening the papers in front of him. The professor seemed harmless enough, and Peter did feel comfortable with him. So he began his story. "Well, just to give you an idea, shortly after buying the company, I went to meet with the president of Magic's largest customer. I introduced myself as Magic's new owner and told him that I was calling on our customers to get acquainted. I wanted to get more of their business. He burst out laughing, and asked, 'Why would you want more of my business when you can't even handle the business you've got?'"

"What did you do?" Keen asked.

"I didn't know what he was talking about," admitted Peter. "Then he told me that we're always late with his orders. And he said that if he could get the parts somewhere else at the same price or for even a little more money, he would. He assured me that he had nothing against me personally. It's just that he didn't think we knew our asses from our elbows. He told me that I was not the only supplier who was continually late. When I got back to the plant, I asked to see the past-due schedule. Guess what?"

Keen did not even hazard a guess.

"We didn't *have* a past-due schedule. Guess what else we didn't have? We didn't even have a good way to figure our past-due schedule. We had no computers and were missing a lot of other tools. In fact, the closest thing we had to an electronic device or computer was a typewriter. So, we manually figured all of our deliveries and past-dues. And do you know what we found?"

By now, Keen knew that he did not need to say anything.

"Our on-time deliveries were running at about 55 to 60 percent. After the revelation about our delivery time, I decided to use a critical eye and take stock of any other evident problems. And that's when I discovered a whole lot of other problems. I call them problems now, but they're common occurrences in most manufacturing plants—or maybe I should say opportunities."

This statement surprised Keen. "Most manufacturing plants have major problems?"

"They sure do. And I can say that with confidence because I've been in manufacturing for thirty years, holding many jobs, mostly as a manufacturing engineer, plant manager and general manager, including a division presidency with a major U.S. corporation, and now as an owner. Now that I'm running a small manufacturing operation on my own, I'm seeing things differently. When you're working in these plants, you get accustomed to how things run and you tend to overlook these kinds of problems. Or maybe you just tend to compensate for them. I do know, though, that you don't even view them as problems. They're just part of the way things have always been."

Keen was digesting all that he just heard. At this point, he decided to administer a dose of theoretical wisdom. As tactfully as possible, the professor asked Peter if he knew the prerequisites to common sense.

Peter wondered what this crazy professor, practically a stranger, had in mind. "I don't know what you're driving at."

"I've studied traditional management techniques of American companies and have found that there are two basic ideas," said Keen in his academic voice. "First, too many managers brag about how their lead times have been reduced, their due date performance has increased, they have reduced scrap, implemented quality programs, provided training for their people, and they have purchased new technologies, and then when they are asked about their profits there is a silence. Profits have not changed and in some cases have gone down. This is what I refer to as the 'legend of the mind managers.' In other words, only in the managers' minds are good things happening. And the first prerequisite of common sense is to have the courage to face reality as it is. This you have just done. Congratulations. Current reality is hard to face."

"Now that you mention it," Peter said, immersed in thought, "I know several companies that fit that profile." He scratched his chin and realized how true the professor's theory was. "What's the second prerequisite?"

"Would you believe me if I said it was to be extremely careful with the use of words?"

Peter immediately replied, "You bet I would. It seems that people are always interpreting things in a different way or don't even understand what the point is."

The professor smiled and said, "We'll have to change that here."

"How?"

"There isn't a condensed version of 'how,' but we'll discuss it soon." Keen then began digging in his briefcase. "I want to write down the problems that you just mentioned before I forget them. I teach because I'm absent-minded."

As the professor began recording the problems identified so far, Peter looked at his watch and told Keen that he had to get back to work. But he promised they would talk about the other problems soon.

"Am I invited to the meeting at the end of the day?" asked Keen.

"I was planning on seeing you here at 4:30." Peter wanted to talk longer, but could not because his return phone calls list was getting too long. And he knew many of the calls were from customers who needed answers on either quality or delivery. It seemed like all his time these days was spent on such calls.

When Peter got back to his office, he began to wonder if Keen was too theoretical and if he would be able to relate to the practical side of managing a business. But he recalled that Dr. Deming had said, "Theory and practice had to be forged together if an organization wanted to be successful."

Peter thought of the dangerous path Magic was taking. Its sales and profits were going downhill. And more recently, he was feeling barraged with increased customer pressures. 'What do I have to lose in the short run by taking a chance with Keen?' he mumbled to himself.

3

Start with Basic Problems

"Treat People Like You Want to Be Treated, and Never Ask Anyone to Do Something That You Wouldn't Do Yourself"

Keen was the first one in the room. It was 4:28. He believed that *one shouldn't reward people for being late by waiting for them.* And he practiced what he taught. A few minutes later, almost everyone else had arrived for the meeting.

Before starting the video, Peter stood up and addressed the group. "JIT will offer us the potential for eliminating or sharply reducing the waste in our plant," he told the group. "It will also help us to reduce incoming inspections, paper processing associated with deliveries and shipments, the amount of detailed production scheduling that is currently required, and all of the detailed tracking associated with our present control system. At first, everyone may want to look only at the hard work involved, but it will eventually make everybody's job easier."

Brian Gower, plant supervisor, was particularly impressed with JIT. He commented that he had never before realized the importance of plant layout. But he could see that the layout of a plant was much different with JIT, because inventory was constantly moving on the shop floor and was not put in a storeroom between processes.

The entire group seemed more interested in the video this afternoon. Their eyes left the screen only when they took notes. Their questions and comments revealed that they understood what they had watched. Several people were discussing JIT on their way out the door at the conclusion of the meeting.

After the meeting, Keen again stayed behind with Peter. "OK," said Keen. "What were some of your other problems?"

Peter got out a list he had prepared during the day in anticipation of this question by the professor.

"Are you ready?" Peter asked. "Number one: The layout of the plant is terrible. Over the past thirty years, the building has gone through several additions and expansions. So the layout of the aisles and the plant has been set, and everyone's simply gotten used to it. But it's definitely not the most efficient layout. And speaking of aisles, we don't have aisles that a high-low can go through. So I began to examine the possibility of changing our aisles in some way, but I didn't know exactly what to do."

Keen was busy writing.

"We're trying to correct this problem, but it's not going as smoothly as I had hoped." There was a pause.

"Number two: We don't have adequate racks. And the racks that we do have are stacked full of unneeded inventory. Number three: Our old equipment is breaking down frequently, which makes it very difficult for us to maintain competitive lead times. Sometimes we have more machines down than we do in operation. Number four: Much of our equipment is running at capacity. So we don't have any equipment available to manufacture more parts. Number five: Poor material handling. Number six: There was no quality program in place, and there is no quality manual being used. That's why we're having these sessions. I want our supervisors to be aware of the various concepts."

"Whoa, whoa," said Keen. Peter was talking faster than the professor could write.

Peter waited until Keen was finished writing, then he continued. "We have no engineers. We also didn't have an up-to-date employee handbook or set of company policies. I've been working on the handbook for the past two months. I should be finished within the next few weeks."

Talking all this out was therapy for Peter. He knew there were things wrong with his company, but he had not yet written everything down to be analyzed. "And there's more. The plant was extremely dirty and crowded. Housekeeping used to be almost nonexistent."

Keen caught the key words and asked, "Used to be?"

"That's right. Early on I took measures to correct this. And we're starting to see a little improvement in housekeeping, safety, and quality. Maybe not down here in the basement yet. But definitely up on the shop floor. In fact, the first person I had to let go after buying the company was the quality manager, because he didn't believe in either people or quality. I try to work with people—I try very hard to work with people—but in this process some people are going to fall by the wayside."

"What did you do to call attention to housekeeping?"

Peter smiled.

"Well, it kind of came about by accident," he admitted. "I've always been a bear when it comes to housekeeping. And some of the workers came in early one day and saw me mopping and cleaning their bathroom."

"You were scrubbing the bathroom?"

"Yes. We had a couple of people here who were very weak in their job performance. And one of them was our janitor. He refused to do his job, and we had to let him go. So until we found a new janitor, I took on the chore because housekeeping has always been extremely important to me. Basically, I just took over cleaning the bathrooms until we eventually found somebody."

"Why did you do it?"

"Because I believe in two principles, and I have told everybody these two principles from day one. The first one is, *treat people as you want to be treated,* and the second one is, *never ask somebody to do something that you wouldn't do yourself.* I can recall a couple of occasions where we had to work Sundays. Well, I believe that management should be here too. So I came in, but since I couldn't set up four-slide machines—I can set up other machines, but not these—I'd be here on Sunday mornings wiping down these oily machines and mopping the floor. Sunday was a rare workday, but once in a while we had to do it."

"So you became a role model for them."

Peter simply shrugged and said, "Isn't that management's job? I do know that a lot of them began cleaning up after themselves in the bathroom and even in their work areas. After all," Peter continued, "*you can't expect somebody to do something if they don't know what you want or if they don't know how to do it.*"

As Keen listened to Peter he could see the possibilities of Magic's efforts transcending all boundaries. The principles could be used in manufacturing plants, corporate offices, schools, even at home. If people learned the principles at work or school, they would carry over into their personal lives.

"I'm curious about something," asked the professor. "Did you make it clear to the workers that housekeeping was an expectation?"

"Yes, I did that all the time. I still do it. I believe that workers need to know—and they want to know—what is expected. But it's how you go about it that counts."

Keen thought about the events that Peter had just described. This was not something you read about in textbooks. In all of the books he had studied in the various business courses, not one had suggested that the CEO should clean the toilets in order to set an example. And he had never seen this mentioned in any of the case studies that he read.

Peter stopped and looked at the professor, who was sitting in front of his notepad with a blank look on his face. "John, you haven't written down the last couple of items. Is anything wrong?"

"Well, why did you buy it?"

"Buy what?"

"Last week you told me about the special cables becoming obsolete, which will cost you millions of dollars in revenue. This morning you revealed that your company had a 60 percent on-time delivery. And now you've told me about all of these problems, some of which seem to be quite serious." Keen hesitated before repeating the question. "Why did you buy this company?"

Peter's face took on a look of determination. He looked directly at Keen. "There were many things this company didn't have when I bought it. To tell you the truth, though, I didn't recognize most of these problems at the time because they're so common in most manufacturing plants." Peter paused. "The one thing this company did have was an energetic and receptive workforce. I could just tell that they would be receptive to new ideas. Plus, I thought it was profitable."

"Do you still believe that your workforce is receptive and energetic?"

"Yes, I do. From my background I knew what was required of a manufacturing company in the automotive industry. And I saw from the beginning that we were fumbling. Since buying Magic, I've had several meetings with everyone in the whole plant. In one of our first meetings, I started sharing with everybody what we were going to be doing in the future. I provided them with my vision for the future. I explained to them that at that time our quality system had to improve, that we weren't doing any SPC, that we were kind of in the dark ages in housekeeping and in many other things. I wanted them to know that they didn't have to be afraid of new concepts. I hired a person to start teaching our people SPC, while we began to develop a quality manual."

"You started all of this shortly after buying the company?"

"Yes I did. My vision when I first came to Magic was *to be the best at what we did*—or, as I'm finding out now, to be a world-class manufacturing company. I brought that vision, that concept, to Magic and I would not let go of it. My goal was not to become a huge corporation. When I came to Magic, I didn't even know the term *world-class,* but I knew I wanted to be the best."

"So you identified some of the major problems quite early? And you've tried to take some steps to correct them? You also shared your vision of Magic with all the workers. Do you feel this is important for the workers to know?"

Peter nodded. "Definitely. We all need to be going in the same direction—the right direction." Just then, the intercom came on, announcing an important call for Peter. He excused himself and left the room. Keen was left alone with his thoughts.

4

Academician Learns from the Practitioner

*"We Have to Listen to All The Gurus and Then Implement
What Is Applicable to Us"*

It had been only a few months since Keen had met Peter, and many of the
lessons and concepts introduced at Magic were beginning to make a difference. The workers were excited about learning new techniques and
applying them to their jobs. But Keen wanted to have more of an impact.
He did not want only to participate in the discussions; he wanted to get in
the trenches with everyone else. After all, he was starting to feel very comfortable on the shop floor.

As Keen was walking down an aisle, he noticed that the shelves were piled
high with boxes. In fact, an entire wall was filled with the cartons. He looked
inside several of the boxes and saw finished goods. This took him by surprise,
because during the past several sessions he and everyone at Magic had been
discussing ways to reduce inventory. Two features in particular—improved
quality and reduced inventory—were goals that Magic was pursuing.

Keen could not believe it. How could no one else in this entire company
not have noticed this excess inventory? Why did it take a university professor to discover the problem? And he had not only found the problem, but
he also knew the solution.

He walked briskly to Peter's office and asked Peter to follow him. Peter
did not have time for this interruption in today's schedule, but the urgency
in Keen's request made the situation seem like an emergency. Upon entering the aisle, Keen pointed to the stacks of boxes on the shelves. "What are
those?" he asked.

"This is why you dragged me across the plant?"

"Please, Peter. What is in all of those boxes?"

"Parts."

Then the professor stepped up onto the proverbial soapbox. "Peter, you,
of all people, should know better."

"What do you mean? I don't have time for any games today."

"None of these finished goods should be here. You know that. I know that. These parts should all be gone."

Peter was perturbed. "But these springs are only worth 1/2 cent apiece and—"

Keen cut him off. "That doesn't matter. You've been in the last several sessions. Haven't we agreed that we need to lower our inventories and—"

Now Peter interrupted Keen. "Wait a minute. Wait just one minute. Look at these shelves. How many boxes of parts would you say we have there?"

"Fifty-six," Keen declared. "I counted them earlier."

"Okay. We have fifty-six boxes of springs stacked against that wall. Now, can you guess what the total value of those fifty-six boxes is?"

The professor looked at the inventory. "Well, that's a lot of space. My calculation would be at least a few thousand dollars. Maybe more."

"No," said Peter. "It's more like a few hundred dollars, and the space represents less than two hundred square feet."

Keen was surprised. He had not known the value of the parts. He looked at Peter. Then, in disbelief, he looked back at the boxes.

Peter held his composure and explained why the fifty-six boxes were on the shelves. "Our inventory cost is practically all in raw material and work-in-process (WIP). So what we want to do is lower our raw material and WIP. When you're talking penny parts that don't take up much space, it's all right to carry finished goods as long as you've got quality parts and know that the customer will eventually purchase the parts."

Keen held up his hand to stop Peter in midsentence and quoted a statement from a video they had seen at a recent meeting. "Remember, in JIT you try not to carry inventory."

Peter did not have time for textbooks and theories today. "In most cases, that is true. But sometimes theories don't work in the real world. Look at those boxes. There's little cost, there's little storage space used, and there's no spoilage factor. Now keeping these boxes of parts in our plant may set us slightly away from complete or perfect JIT, but it suits our specific needs."

"But the tapes that we watched stated that—"

"Stop right there. I don't care what was said on the tape. In most situations, theories are correct. But we can't just copy one guru or concept. If we want to be world-class, *we have to listen to all of the gurus and then take what specifically applies to us.* Now if we were making expensive items that took up a lot of storage space, then we would have to control our finished goods inventory. But in a situation like ours, when we can get small parts—say ten thousand to a box—and our customer, who happens to be a very good customer, wants only two thousand a month, then it's dumb to do the setup every month, especially when a setup can take up to eight hours. You run these jobs ahead of time. What you set up frequently are your high-volume jobs."

Peter paused to make certain that the professor was keeping up with him, then continued, "Not everything can be learned from one expert's video or workbook. What he or she is teaching is theoretically correct, but sometimes certain variations have to be made for particular applications or specific situations."

The professor realized that he was not the only teacher in this plant. A moment ago, the academician was going to teach the practitioner how to solve an obvious problem. But instead the academician became the student, and he discovered that the problem was actually not a problem. In reality, storing the boxes of finished goods was a wise business decision. Professor John Keen had just received his first experiential learning dividend from the synthesis of theory and practice.

5

Grow People First

*"How Can Anyone Grow If We Don't Cultivate
the Whole Person?"*

During the short time since John Keen had first visited Magic, he had sat in on many sessions and had been involved in many discussions on the shop floor. Theoretically, he had already been exposed to practically everything brought up in the meetings about JIT, SPC, quality management, world-class manufacturing, and the other popular management theories that dominated many managers' thinking.

Keen recognized that all of the various concepts would work if introduced and applied properly. But he noticed that the philosophies focused more on production techniques than on growing individuals. Then, in today's session, Keen had hit upon a missing element. He realized that management must first focus on improving the personal, professional, social, and spiritual quality of employees' lives before focusing on any of the quality initiatives based on some type of a statistical tool or management philosophy and technique.

Upon realizing this, he could not contain himself and blurted out, "An organization that grows people first will establish a culture that will make the acceptance and implementation of other changes easier."

Peter and the others looked up from their papers. They thought the professor had gone crazy. For a moment, Keen wished that he had withheld his revelation, at least until he had more evidence. But how could he get any evidence if he could not implement his idea in an actual working environment? He realized that Magic was moving in the right direction—with lots of lunches for specific events, frequent safety and quality meetings, plenty of plantwide communications meetings and SPC training, and so forth.

Looking around the table, Keen rested his gaze on Peter. "We've been studying several different concepts. What do all of them focus on?"

"Production techniques," said Fred Ulrich, the plant manager.

21

"Right!" Keen rejoiced, using his hands and body in the reply. "And in order to implement these techniques, we must have the cooperation and understanding of the people. Right?"

Peter was cautiously looking at his new friend. He had never seen him behave like this before. Slowly, he answered, "Right."

"In order to do that, wouldn't the people be more receptive and effective if we took time to grow them?"

"Grow? Grow them?" one of the supervisors asked. A few others in the room also repeated the words.

Keen was beginning to lose his audience. "We need to focus on improving the personal, professional, social, and spiritual quality of the employees' lives before we can focus on JIT, quality issues, or any other type of management-based initiative, and before we can help our customers."

All eyes were on the professor.

"When was the last time you dug half a hole?" Keen asked.

There were a few moments of silence and then some laughter. Someone started to explain how this was possible. Then more laughter erupted.

The professor asked another question. "Haven't we all heard that we are basically made up of mind, body, and soul?" Before anyone could answer, Keen went on to state that some managers treat only parts of people. "So, how can we grow anyone if we don't cultivate the whole person?" he asked. "What happens if we cut a seed into pieces? We're not sure what we'll get."

Most of the people in the room were confused.

"How many managers ask workers to bring all their brawn—their bodies—and only some of their brain power—their minds—to work? How many managers ask workers to check their souls and their brains at the door? How can we grow a whole person when they are dissected into pieces?"

Everyone listened and could see the sense of the statement. He asked, "How do we accomplish this feat of improving the personal, professional, social, and spiritual quality of everyone's lives?"

There were no responses.

"We're already doing a lot," said Keen. "Maybe you just have to formalize it some more. But you need to concentrate on the soft sciences."

"Soft sciences?" someone sarcastically repeated.

It was too late for Keen to stop, so he explained. "Well, during the past couple of years, I've done some research on how things can be broken down into hard sciences and soft sciences. Hard sciences include JIT, TQM and the other world-class production techniques that we're learning about. The soft sciences are your quality of life issues. For example, a person's self-esteem, how you introduce change, how you handle discipline, and so on."

The group was trying to understand everything they were hearing. They had not expected the session to take such a turn like this.

Peter noticed that everyone in the room seemed to be interested in what the professor was saying. Now, if they just agreed with some of it.

"*How many people come to work to intentionally do something wrong?*" Keen asked.

The immediate response from the group was "none."

"Then how come we have scrap, rework, customer complaints, machine breakdowns, wrong parts shipped, and so forth?"

Nobody had an answer.

Keen continued by directing a question at Fred Ulrich, "Do you think the workers would be proud of improved quality in their products and jobs?"

"I know they would."

"*How many of you are against quality?* Please raise your hands," Keen asked.

No one raised a hand. The professor then said that since everyone in the room wanted to buy quality products and services, they also had an obligation to provide the same thing for Magic's customers.

Peter and the others could have heard a pin drop. They knew this was exactly what they wanted to do, but wondered how they could accomplish such a mission impossible. Keen hesitated and gathered his thoughts. "When thinking of quality, we usually think in terms of product quality. Is that right?"

"Of course."

"Well, nothing could be more wrong."

This statement caused a slight murmur in the room. A few of the supervisors exchanged glances. The professor was beginning to walk on thin ice. He had to think fast. "In total quality management, the first and foremost concern should not be with product quality but rather with the quality of employees' lives."

Ulrich was lost. Peter just gave Keen one of his trademark looks.

"If you study the most successful quality situations, you'll find that instilling quality into the people has always been the first fundamental principle of TQM," Keen pointed out. "Or to paraphrase, if you can build quality into your people, then you're already halfway toward producing quality products."

"I see where you're going," Peter said. "Ed Deming, the quality guru who assisted the Japanese in becoming an industrial power, warned us over and over that management must first address the quality of life issues of its workers. Too many American firms jumped directly to SPC techniques or quality circles in the 1970s and 1980s, and they've learned that it does not just automatically take root in the organization. I've seen several firms that are on their third time around, teaching the same personnel the same SPC. They jump into fads and expect instant gratification. They want quick results."

"That's right," said Keen. "But if the quality of life issues are addressed, then workers more readily accept change as a way of life and not as a fad."

Today's meeting had been unique. After everyone left, Keen and Peter began to talk. "When you started taking measures to clean up this plant, you didn't demand that people clean up their work area," said Keen. "You didn't complain because you had to clean up after them in the bathroom, did you?"

Peter just sat quietly and listened.

"You didn't yell at anyone. You used soft words, not hard words."

"Soft words? Hard words?"

"You used the soft sciences without even realizing it. Don't you see?"

"See what?"

Keen tried to find the correct words to explain what he meant. "With hard words, you threaten, you scream, you belittle, and you lessen a person's self-esteem. You put them on the defensive. They hear but don't listen, and they do only what they are told and no more. With soft words, you maintain or enhance a person's self-esteem and you get much more accomplished. You create a more cooperative environment. And the way you handled the housekeeping was mostly with a soft touch."

"Well, sometimes I did it in a soft way. But when they wouldn't pick up or clean up after I told them umpteen times, I would resort to the hard way."

They both laughed.

"Did you begin to see any other benefits after housekeeping in the plant started to improve?" asked the professor.

Peter thought for a moment. "As a matter of fact we did. Even after I hired the new janitor, everyone continued to pitch in to keep the bathrooms clean. And shortly afterwards I noticed our cleaning efforts began to move into other areas. I also noticed that people began to pick up after themselves in the eating area."

"Anything else?"

"Well, just recently, I've noticed that more and more people are picking up in their own individual work areas. In fact, I've seen several people take a broom to their area, and they're even beginning to reach out onto the shop floor. We've also started straightening up the aisles and the racks."

"Anything else?"

"Yes, as a matter of fact, there is," Peter said with pride. "I've had a few people suggest that we take a close look at our lighting. We haven't done much with our lighting yet, but we've just started looking into it. Little by little, I'm starting to see things turn around as far as pride in housekeeping. Some progress is being made. I hope the progress will be fast enough to start making a profit." Peter sat back in his chair. "Anything else?"

Keen grinned. "Well, from what I've seen, you are very involved with all of your people. You're much more involved than any other manager or president I know or have read about. One cannot leave people alone and expect them to grow without involvement, just like a seed won't grow unless you nurture and attend to it. Remember that movie about 'build your field of dreams and they will come?' I'm not sure of that particular dream in reality, but I feel confident that profits will come to Magic because of your intense involvement with the quality of life for your people."

"I'm counting on it. We're operating at the break-even point. Our sales are dropping and profits have disappeared."

"But there has to be a strong correlation between involvement and profits," Keen pointed out. "Just look at the facts. The workers have taken pride in the work areas and in the general housekeeping throughout the plant. Right? And they've done this without the threat of losing their jobs, and without the promise of a raise. Right?"

Peter was beginning to see where the professor was taking this point.

"And you have to believe that if they did it with housekeeping, they'll do it with most other aspects of their jobs."

Peter looked at Keen and a smile grew across his face. "That's right. But it is not quite that easy."

6

Weakest Link

"If You Focus on Everything, You Focus on Nothing." Plato

Peter liked the idea of bringing a university classroom atmosphere and stature to his people. He believed it was good to listen to outside influences, people with credentials who affirm the concepts that everyone is learning. Peter also believed it added to the credibility of what they were trying to do at Magic. Moreover, he knew it was good to talk 'up' to people rather than 'down.'

When Peter asked Keen to take the lead at the next meeting, the professor was thrilled beyond words. Up until now, most of the meetings had involved watching videotapes, listening to audiotapes, or working in workbooks. For several of the sessions, Peter had brought in special guest speakers to talk to the group. The guest speakers were all experts in various aspects of manufacturing.

That is why most everyone in the room was surprised to see Keen stand up to lead today's meeting, especially after what had happened the previous morning.

It seems the professor had stopped by yesterday to talk to Peter, who was in a meeting with some customers who were irate because of a late order. So, Keen had decided to pass the time by taking a walk around the shop floor. During his stroll, he had found the work crew responsible for the botched job that Peter was trying to explain. The workers and supervisors were arguing among themselves and passing the blame to one another. Keen had listened to their accusations. At that point he had ended up ruffling a few feathers by expounding some of his theories. The last thing they had wanted to hear was the professor's opinions of how to improve operations. They could not believe that he viewed a fixed schedule as being practical. And his idea of reducing setup times from hours to minutes had seemed utterly preposterous to them.

27

Just when some of the workers and supervisors had been thinking of jettisoning Keen, Peter had happened to come into the room. He had reached an agreement with the customers and wanted to explain the arrangement to the workers. He had overheard some of the discussion, and had paused to listen. He had asked bluntly, "Who cares if setup time is minutes or hours as long as we are moving in the right direction?" A few of the workers had grumbled in agreement.

He had then pointed out that if it currently took four hours for a setup, then the goal should be to move it down to three hours and then to two hours and so forth. He agreed with the workers and supervisors that they might never be able to set up in minutes, but knew they had to start thinking in terms of how they might continuously improve.

"We have to change our paradigms," he had explained. "We need to think of ways to build tools differently—think about ways of changing how our machines operate—continuously be thinking about all kinds of changes. You and I have to be paradigm pioneers."

Peter had continued, "For now, we need to make sure that everyone is ready for each setup and that we eliminate wasted steps in the setup process. I believe if we can do these things, we can cut setup time in half."

The atmosphere had seemed to relax and the workers had seemed to accept Keen's statement regarding a single minute exchange of die. Their ears were open again. Word of the discussion had spread rapidly throughout the plant.

The group at today's meeting felt that even if some of Keen's theories seemed slightly unorthodox, he did demonstrate that he was sincerely interested in the success of Magic. And maybe some of his ideas were not based on total lunacy.

During the past months, most of the workers and managers had come to feel comfortable with Keen. And yesterday's discussion had not changed their feelings toward him. After all, he had just been trying to help.

Keen smiled at the group and jumped into the meeting. "At the last session, I talked a little about the soft sciences and growing people," he reminded everyone. "And I probably confused some of you—"

"What else is new?" someone jokingly mumbled from the back of the room.

Keen looked in the direction of the comment and smiled. He saw the humor in the remark. "Where was I?" he asked as he rubbed his head. "Oh, soft sciences and growing people. I thought I would start out by telling you a parable that I heard a few years ago.

"The Chinese bamboo seed is a nut with a very tough skin. After it's planted, it must be watered and fertilized. But during the first year nothing happens. The second year, it's watered and fertilized again. Yet, once again, nothing happens. The same process is repeated through the third and fourth years. Still, nothing happens. Then during the fifth year, the stalk bursts through the ground, and within a period lasting no more than six weeks, the bamboo grows ninety feet."

Keen looked at all of the faces. He saw a lot of blank stares. "Did the bamboo grow ninety feet in six weeks, or did it grow ninety feet in five years?" he asked.

The room was quiet. "Hello," the professor whispered to the group. They laughed, and finally someone said, "Six weeks."

Chet Franklin, the general manager, then piped up with his response. "I'm a gardener. And I would have to say that five years is probably more accurate."

"Why is that?"

"Because at any time during the interval, if you hadn't maintained the fertilizing and watering, the plant would have died. It's like when you plant a tree—the first year it sleeps, the second year it creeps, and the third year it leaps!"

A smile came across Keen's face. "Good observation. And that's very similar to growing people. Or to growing a healthy climate in an organization. You can't expect miracles to happen overnight."

"So what is the moral of the story?" asked Chet.

"I can see a couple," said Kevin, an assembly department supervisor. "Management and most people think only about short-term results. They focus only on this quarter's earnings. Don't get me wrong. That's important, but we need to also have long-range plans."

Fred Ulrich had another observation. "I agree with you. But what I've seen happen time and time again is that when programs don't produce immediate results, they are abandoned, even though in the long run they would have proven quite profitable and effective."

"Well, no one wants to be responsible for long-range ideas," said Chet. "Everyone feels that if they make a mistake they'll be condemned. They know they have to produce quick results."

Keen made his own observation. "If we want this entire organization to operate more productively, to change longstanding attitudes and behaviors, the required changes may require nurturing for months and years. Are you willing to make that commitment? Are you willing to use the soft sciences? Are you willing to help people grow?"

"We are!" said the group.

Peter pushed his chair back slightly and everyone in the room turned their attention to him. They respected Peter and his integrity. "If we make this commitment, people will benefit not only from a job standpoint but also in their personal lives," he commented. "And once the effects take hold here at Magic, I believe the results will be measured in increased job satisfaction and security as well as in knowing that Magic is financially stable. Not only will our employees be happy about participating in our financial success, but they will be very proud to say that they work at Magic.

The group was enthused. Slightly confused, but extremely enthused. The professor thought to himself before going on to the next topic how Peter had the gift of always being able to communicate his vision to everyone. He did it with sincerity, feeling, and clarity, and straight from the heart.

"I learned a couple of weeks ago that most manufacturing plants overlook—or compensate for—the various problems in their operations," Keen commented. Peter remembered saying that and smiled. The others had no idea what Keen meant.

"We know that JIT, TQM, and the other concepts work," continued the professor. "We've seen films about their successes, and we've witnessed dozens of successful case studies. So that's a given, these concepts do work! It's just that in some organizations they work more effectively than in others. Why is that?"

No one had an answer. Then Keen continued, "Perhaps we should look at this from a different perspective. *How do you measure the strength of a chain?*"

Someone eventually suggested, "By its weakest link."

"That's correct," Keen loudly exclaimed. "The weakest link can be a department in a company, a machine, a work cell, or it can be the people within a department. And your goal is not to get rid of your weakest link but to work to strengthen it. You don't necessarily have to fire that person or that whole department, but you have to find a way to bolster it."

The professor paused and took a sip of water. "What happens to Magic's competitive strength if it should focus its limited amount of time, energy, and resources on a strong link?"

After a period of silence, a voice hesitantly commented, "Not that much."

Keen was pleased. "So we should first identify our weakest link. We need to find that which is constraining us the most from making more money in an ethical way. This is the first step in the Theory of Constraints (TOC). Do you remember what Plato reminded us of regarding this point? If you focus on everything, you focus on nothing. But let's take it one step further. We must not only focus, but we need to focus on our weakest link."

Peter realized where Keen was heading, and he added, "Our strengths are taking care of themselves. Businesses larger than ours, even major corporations, for that matter, have failed because they did not focus on their weaknesses. No matter how big a company is, there are just so many resources of time, people, and working capital."

Thinking to himself, Peter realized that until recently he had been focusing on everything, and consequently not a lot had been accomplished. 'But,' he wondered to himself, 'what should Magic be focusing on at this time?'

Keen continued, "We need to identify our weaknesses and improve them before we can expect major improvement throughout the organization. And we need to find our primary weaknesses."

"How?" someone asked.

Peter jumped in. "Let's close this meeting on that note. I want each of you to think of all of the problems and concerns you see that need to be improved at Magic. No matter how obvious or how small. Write them down. Look at them. Is there a common denominator? Then, on Friday we'll have a meeting and compare notes."

7

Fix the Problem, Not the Blame

"The Problem with Many Organizations Is That They Over-Managed and Under-Led"

Most everyone brought a list of weak links to Friday's meeting. Some of the lists contained only a couple of problems, while others had ten or more. After more than two hours of intense discussion and brainstorming, the group still could not come up with any viable conclusions. But then Peter noticed that maybe they had made some progress.

"We're trying to find areas where there is some major concern, right?" he asked. "And we've brought up dozens, if not hundreds of topics. For example, we discussed housekeeping. Then we dismissed it. Why did we dismiss it?"

No response.

"Let's list it," Peter continued. "After all, it is a major concern. Our housekeeping may have improved, but there is still a lot of work to do. Clean restrooms, clean work areas, clean aisles, and a clean shop floor can go a long way to boost morale. Improved housekeeping will also give people pride in their jobs and in *their* company. Housekeeping is something we should always be concerned about. He thought to himself, 'I wonder if this is a part of what Dr. Deming meant about theory and practice? There are no "ands" or "buts" about it. We will do it. We have to do it to survive, and to provide jobs into the twenty-first century.'

The professor stood up and wrote on the transparency that one problem was HOUSEKEEPING. As he stood there he began rubbing his bald forehead and asked if anyone remembered anything about a weakest link.

Several mumbled, "Yes."

"Does this concept apply at this time?" Keen asked.

"Yea, I think it does," said Chris from the press room. "I'm trying to remember exactly what you said the other day." Chris paused as he gathered his thoughts. "You said that unless we strengthened our weakest link Magic would not be gaining much in the long run."

33

Chris was gaining more and more self-confidence and feeling better about himself after every answer. This quiet young man was even beginning to enjoy speaking in meetings. Until recently, he had trouble talking to a group of two. Now, he was standing up and addressing the entire room.

"I guess we should choose the ideas that will strengthen Magic the most at this time," suggested Chris.

"What about preventive maintenance?" asked Larry, the maintenance supervisor. Larry was a quiet man, and no one could believe that he had joined the discussion.

"Why? You trying to get out of some work?" someone joked.

"No, but if everyone learns a little more about preventive maintenance, we'll have less downtime, less scrap, and more productivity. Do you wait until your car breaks down, stranding you in the middle of nowhere? Or do you take it into a garage at the first sign that something might be wrong?"

"What can we do? I don't know anything about repairing these machines," was the general sentiment of everyone in the room. But Peter and Keen saw more. They saw a maintenance person concerned about customers.

"I thought of that," responded Larry. "Maybe we could prepare a schedule for preventive maintenance to be done in each department on a daily, weekly, and monthly basis. This won't be done by the maintenance department but by the workers in each department. I could show them what to do, and leave some detailed instructions so they remember everything."

Peter was impressed. "Does everyone agree that preventive maintenance is important?"

No one could argue with Larry's statement. Fred Ulrich thought of a twist. "Perhaps we could even publish a monthly report on all of the various maintenance costs for each machine in each department?"

Keen was smiling as he wrote on the board that the second problem was PREVENTIVE MAINTENANCE. "How many workers like to wait for someone to fix their machines?" he asked.

"Not many," was the reply.

Peter jumped in and said, "Workers come to work wanting to be productive, and it is up to management to provide them the support and the tools they need to do their job."

"Could preventive maintenance and predictive maintenance be considered a quality of life issue?" Keen asked.

After a few moments Peter spoke up, "I think that what the professor is trying to tell us is that if the worker has the right tools and the machines are always working, then we can go home at the end of the day with a sense that we've done something." He glanced at Keen, who was nodding in agreement. "If not, then we go home frustrated because the machine breakdowns have put pressure on us to ship at any cost. This hurts our quality, increases our costs, and certainly doesn't make it fun to come to work the next day. If we get our machines and tools in proper order, then we won't have this constant daily pressure of hot, hotter, hottest. We will also be able to lower the scheduling pressures."

Peter could tell by the expressions in the room that everyone understood. He turned to Larry. "We need to work on this. Thank you for the suggestion."

Another problem discussed during the meeting was purchased materials. Most of the supervisors had the same problem. Their workers were frequently getting inferior materials from certain suppliers. And, in the course of the discussion, it became clear that no one was doing anything about it. The same two suppliers' names kept popping up.

Since beginning the JIT system, supplier relations had radically changed. Each of the suppliers had been asked to make more frequent deliveries, which required changes in shipping procedures. Some of them had balked at this request and caused serious problems in the process. It was becoming evident that new suppliers might be required in order to effectively implement the new JIT procedures.

Keen wrote that number three was MATERIAL PROBLEMS.

The final problem was common to practically every department, as well as most every manufacturing company—lengthy setup times. Setup times need to be reduced—especially for any constrained resource—because indirectly or directly they had an impact on delivery time, amount of investment needed, length of lead times, quality of parts, and lower inventories. Of course, TQM, preventive maintenance, good materials, and good suppliers also needed to be in place.

Keen wrote that number four was SETUP TIME REDUCTION.

The group was pleased with its progress. They had identified four problems in the company. And they knew that if they could get a handle on these problems, they would be able to make a significant impact on the overall operation.

"OK. Let's look at each of these items individually and then as a group," said Peter.

"Well, the only common denominator I can see is the people," someone commented.

Neither Keen nor Peter had even thought of this. They looked at each other, and then Peter asked, "Is there anything then that people are doing, or aren't doing, that would cause each of these problems to occur?"

The room was silent.

"Does everyone on the shop floor know what's expected of them?" Keen asked hesitantly.

One of the supervisors laughed as he said they did.

"Who trained them?" Keen asked.

The same supervisor looked at Keen again, and asked, "What do you mean?"

"Well, does everyone know the best way to do everything associated with their job function?" There was silence. "If they do, did you train them in the most efficient way to do it all? And, is the way they're doing their job necessarily the most effective way?"

No one attempted to answer the professor's question.

"Well, isn't that what we're learning about now with all of the videos and books?" asked another supervisor.

"Not really," said Peter. "We're learning about JIT, TQM, and so on. But we're not learning about specific job functions. And besides, we're only learning the hard sciences in the videos and at the meetings—"

Keen interrupted Peter and blurted out, "Let's take setup time reduction. Why aren't the people able to reduce their setup time?"

This question brought several angry glares from people in the room.

"How much time is spent with the new worker during training?" Keen asked.

Some laughter broke out. A toolmaker thought for a second. "Oh, I guess anywhere from ten to twenty minutes."

"Do you think this is sufficient time?" inquired Keen.

"No," was the response from several people.

"How well does the trainer know the job?" Keen asked.

"Who knows?" was a response from the group.

"Is the trainer current with the best knowledge possible to do the job?"

More shrugs. More silence. Someone mumbled, "Probably not even close to being up to speed."

"What do you tell the worker after this educational process of ten or twenty minutes?" Keen asked.

Chris said, "Come find me if you have any questions or problems."

"Do you think a new worker will come ask you any questions?"

"Probably not," Chris replied. He had never thought of this before.

"How come?" asked the professor.

Question after question. By continually asking questions the workers were inventing the answers and starting to think about what they had to do to get better—to be the best.

Doug from the spring department spoke up and said, "Now that you put it that way, I would guess that she would be afraid to speak up because she wouldn't want to look bad on the job. She wouldn't want to risk being thought of as a slow learner. She also might just not like to talk to that particular trainer."

"Good insight," Keen said. "How long do you think it will take her by this method to become a good worker?" Keen explained that he was not trying to blame anyone for anything or make any accusations. He was simply looking at things as an outsider, as someone who was not as close to the operations and who might see things differently. He brought a new set of eyes to the company.

The professor then said, "*Fix the problem, not the blame.*" This was the first time that anyone had heard Keen say this, but he would later remind them over and over again. He then asked, "What is the problem associated with gradually reducing setup times to several minutes?"

"To tell you the truth I never looked at setup reduction time from that angle," said Fred Ulrich. "I've been here for eleven years and I can tell you that our people have never received any updating of their skills, and some of them were not that well trained in the first place. They're simply doing everything the same way they've always done it. But they do get their job done."

"Isn't operating a machine just like anything else?" Keen asked. "Don't you need to be constantly trained in new production techniques to compete in a more competitive market? Would you let a doctor operate on you who graduated from medical school thirty years ago, had never received any updated training, had never learned another new thing, and still used the same equipment that he was trained on? I wouldn't," said Keen. "And I don't think any of you would either. But isn't that happening in the manufacturing world? Workers start at a job and never receive any updated training, never learn another new thing, never attend any classes, and still use the same equipment that they were trained on."

Ulrich was scratching his chin. "So, most of the problems that we've pointed out can all be attributed to the fact that the workers weren't trained properly and haven't continued to be trained?"

The professor shrugged, and someone asked, "How does that pertain to housekeeping or preventive maintenance?"

"Who trained them in the proper way to clean up their work area, or to organize their work area, or to maintain their machine?" asked Keen.

One of the supervisors asked, "Do you think that after they learn these new concepts they'll improve?"

"To a point," said Peter. "I think teaching the techniques is just the beginning, though. They not only have to learn how the techniques work, but also how to apply them. What we're talking about here is improving a person's personal life as well as his or her professional life. I think that's what we have to do. We have to educate everyone across the board."

Keen stood up and faced the group. "If a workforce is educated properly on a continuous improvement basis, and they have the right tools, will they accomplish their goals?"

"Why wouldn't they?" Ulrich shot back.

"Let me share a short story," said Keen. "Two lumberjacks in the northern woods were arguing over who was better. They decided the only way to resolve the dispute was to have a wood-chopping contest the next day. The rules were that they would start at sunrise, and whoever had cut more wood by sunset would be the winner.

"They began at sunrise the next morning. The first lumberjack worked straight through the day without stopping to rest or eat. The second lumberjack did stop occasionally. So, the first lumberjack was confident of victory.

"Remarkably, at the end of the day the second lumberjack had cut more wood. The first one was stunned. He looked at the first lumberjack and asked, 'How can this be? I worked longer and harder and you stopped to rest. How did you chop more wood?'

"The winning lumberjack replied, 'I did stop several times, but it wasn't to rest. I stopped to sharpen my ax.'"

Keen sat back down. His little parable went a long way. Peter stood up and walked to the front of the room. "I believe that *education is one of our weak links.* If a job is set up wrong, or if the tooling is bad, or if we don't ship on time, or there is a problem in quality, or any one of a hundred different problems—it all comes back to a lack of education. Does everyone here agree that education is a primary weakness?"

"I know it is," said Keen. He then came out with another of his many expressions that made the personnel of Magic think. "*We educate people and we train animals.*"

While Keen had everyone's attention, he explained, "We really need both education and training. Education is the thinking process so important today because of the fast pace of change. The training process is the robotics of life that serve us so well. We automatically do things after once learning them without thinking about them—putting our clothes on and tying our shoestrings. For too long a time companies have stressed employee training that involves teaching workers how to perform a particular job or specific event. In a fast-paced world, the emphasis shifts from training to education. Education increases workers' insights and understanding and teaches the 'why.' At Magic we need to do both. We need to focus on lifelong education for everyone in the organization."

Peter remarked, "Education is the 'why.' Training is the 'how.' And the 'why' should always come first."

"What about all of the tapes we've been watching?" a supervisor asked. "Isn't that considered to be a form of education? Aren't they teaching us the hows and whys?"

"Yes. But that's just the tip of the iceberg," said Keen. "We have to encourage everyone to want more education. And we can't just educate supervisors, we have to educate everyone—about their job, the importance of the quality of their work, world-class manufacturing, eliminating waste, adding value, TQM, JIT, and so forth."

"That'll take forever," someone mumbled.

"No. Not forever," Keen replied. "But it will take time. As Peter said, however, they need to understand how to apply what they learn. Let's take setup time for an example. They need to learn how to look for ways to reduce it on their own. And they won't be able to reduce their setup time if they don't thoroughly understand every aspect of their job or why setup reduction is important."

"And how do you propose we educate them on things we don't even know anything about?" a supervisor asked defensively.

The professor threw out some ideas. "Experts can be called in. Peter has already done this in certain areas. We can watch videos, visit other companies, and brainstorm. We can read books and professional magazines. We can benchmark with other organizations and ask our manufacturing associations to provide us with information.

"Several of you have already attended trade shows and seminars. I am very impressed that two of you have already visited Japan to buy new machinery. It is almost unheard of for a company the size of Magic to pay for someone to go overseas to learn—much less trust someone other than management to make a $100,000 purchase. I know it can be done."

"That will help our workers, but what about us? What about management?" asked another one of the supervisors.

"The supervisors will have to set the examples," said Peter. "I also think that everyone will have to learn how to supervise more effectively." He made this observation without looking at anyone in the group, but it was meant for everyone in the room.

Concern gripped the group. What did Peter mean by that? Before anyone had a chance to ask, the meeting was adjourned by Peter's request for everyone to think about Magic's future.

Peter and Keen stayed after, and Peter began the conversation. "I'm glad we got onto the subject of supervisors, because I think we have a lot of room for improvement. They're receptive, but I think we need to help them improve. Many of them do not know how to hold a meeting, solve a problem, or work as a team."

Keen was quiet and Peter asked him what he thought. "Well, I don't like the words supervisor or supervise. Do you know what supervise means? It means to oversee or to watch. If Magic is going to grow, your supervisors need to be coaches. They need to be leaders."

"I agree."

"Maybe we need to teach them how to lead. I remember hearing someone once say that we must lead others and manage ourselves."

"That makes sense," said Peter. "I've been thinking a lot about the way we're managing here. A business short on capital can borrow money, and one with a poor location can move. But a business short on leadership has little chance for survival. *The problem with many organizations, and especially the ones that are failing, is they tend to be overmanaged and underled. I've seen this in dozens of companies."*

"There is a difference between management and leadership, and both are important. Leadership has to shape and articulate a vision and with the managers establish a mission statement as to how the vision will be managed into reality. In today's reality everyone has to be part leader and part manager. This means one has to accumulate the abilities to coach, teach, guide, direct, motivate, hold people accountable, and accept responsibilities for getting things done. The old days, when the best skilled worker or most liked personality became a manager or leader, are rightfully dying out."

"I think we're on the right track," said Keen. "First of all, we need to identify the necessary leadership qualities. And then we need to cultivate leadership skills."

"How can we do that?"

"Education," Keen said smiling, "We'll educate leaders."

"I don't know if we should call them leaders. Maybe we should call them leads," Peter suggested. "Before we make any definite decisions, however, let's discuss it with the supervisors. We want them to buy into the concept."

The two men put on their coats and headed for the parking lot. As they were walking to their cars to go home for the day, Peter asked Keen if he had anything else on his mind.

Keen replied that he did. "Remember the other day when I mentioned that we needed to start thinking of ways to improve our communications throughout the company? Well, I believe that now is a golden opportunity to start to put a part of it into play."

"What do you have in mind?"

"In the book *The Goal*, written by Eliyahu Goldblatt, there is a character named Herbie."

"I remember him," said Peter. "Wasn't he that fat little boy scout who slowed down the hike?"

"Yes. He was the constraint of that hike process. I suggest that we look for Herbie in Magic by working with all the employees," said Keen. "We already have a good start with the four areas identified by the management team as possible weak links, but shouldn't we involve all the workers?"

"We should."

"I believe we can use a brainstorming format. We can provide a short overview of the significance of what the weakest link idea means and then teach them some basic brainstorming rules."

"Will you handle the facilitating of these sessions?"

"I'd be glad to."

Peter put his hand on the professor's shoulder and smiled. "Hopefully, you can start tomorrow."

As Peter was getting into his car, Chet called to him. "We've got another emergency. Paramount Industries just called. They forgot to order parts. Their assembly lines will be down tomorrow."

"Can we help them?" asked Peter as he got back out of his car.

"There's no material in-house to run the job, and the parts can only run on machine number five, which is already overloaded with jobs due."

"What jobs are in the queue for number five?"

"Unfortunately, a lot of them are for customers that we talked about optimizing," replied Chet.

Magic had been discussing cutting back on their large customer list so as to better serve their good customers. A good customer was one whose management was progressive and reputable, who paid their bills on time, who was willing to work through problems with you as a partner, who was willing to develop and use new technology, who understood and participated in global competition, and who showed promise for more throughput in a growth industry.

Peter rested the palms of his hands on the roof of his car and looked out across the open field beside the parking lot. It seemed so peaceful. He could hear the sounds of birds chirping and a dog barking. The sun was low in the horizon. It was a beautiful evening. He could hear the sounds of several machines inside the plant running at full capacity.

"Optimizing customers and all of that won't help us now with Paramount," said Peter. "Let's both get on the phone and see if we can find the material. You check to see how we can run number five around the clock to get ahead of some of these orders and take care of Paramount."

Peter closed his car door and went back to his office to start making phone calls. Between phone calls he recalled what Dr. Deming had said—*Management creates the systems that cause the workers' frustrations and problems.* "That is exactly what I have done for Magic regarding optimizing our customer list," he thought to himself. "It has been over six months since we discussed which customers didn't meet our customer profile and I agreed to send them a letter explaining to them that they should start to procure a new supplier for their parts. I have just procrastinated in sending letters, and now we are having trouble serving the customers that we want to grow with. I'm causing doubts in the minds of our workers about being honest with optimizing, and we have put ourselves under stress to perform a miracle for a customer we are trying to optimize. We told our key employees that we would be optimizing various jobs after we had consulted with them and their leads, and we haven't delivered. In reality, I have created this problem."

The next day, though, Magic had worked another miracle. The team had found a way to get Paramount its parts.

8

Leads, Not Supervisors

"We Need to Create an Environment Where People Trust Each Other"

P eter, Chet, Fred, and Keen had spent more than a few hours of their own time during the weekend preparing for today's management meeting. Peter especially had considered long and hard how he was going to present to the management of the plant his new idea about leads. "So much is happening here," thought Peter. "So many changes. Is everyone ready? Am I ready? I know that we're doing the right thing, but—." Just then, his thoughts were distracted.

Fred Ulrich and Keen were talking to each other when they came into the room. Peter looked up when he heard their voices. He had asked them to be a little early because he wanted to talk to them. Now the three men were alone around the table.

"This meeting is going to be very important. I just want the two of you to be aware of its significance," said Peter. He seemed troubled. "Regardless of how receptive our workers have been to the various processes and concepts we've introduced, management must take the lead in initiating them. We have to set the example. We have to be involved in the processes, and we have to learn and know TQM, JIT, how to empower people, and any other world-class manufacturing concepts that are applicable for us. That's the only way we're going to get everyone excited about it. We can't just educate people about JIT or TQM, walk away, and expect them to do it."

"I agree," said Ulrich. "But you can't expect our supervisors to accept this new way of managing with open arms. They're going to be hesitant. Even I was skeptical in the beginning. But now I'm able to understand what's going on and how imperative it is."

Peter asked Ulrich if he believed the supervisors would eventually come around.

"In essence, we're asking them to give up the authority that they have worked for years to get. They're supposed to share it with their associates.

This will be a hard concept for some of them to understand—that by giving up their authority, they'll actually have more, because now they'll have the power of everybody working for them solving problems." Ulrich looked down at the table and shook his head. "Sometimes, I even find myself falling back into old patterns."

"It's not going to be easy. I know that," said Peter. "But we can overcome the problems. We'll educate everyone, not just leads. They'll be exposed to classroom training sessions, books, magazine articles, videos, seminars, trade shows, guest speakers, and visits to other firms. We'll bring in trainers and experts. We'll travel around the world to learn, if we have to. We'll do whatever is necessary."

Ulrich still had his doubts. "Do you honestly believe that everyone will accept it?"

The pain was evident in Peter's eyes. "No. I don't believe that everyone will accept it. Quite frankly, I feel we must expect that some of them will fall by the wayside."

He no sooner had completed his sentence when two supervisors came through the door. Soon after, all the supervisors and the others from management were seated around the tables. Peter stood up and began to address them.

"You've noticed many changes taking place here during the past year. We've introduced new concepts and identified some of our major problems. And I believe for the most part that all of the changes have been for the better. Don't you agree?"

Heads nodded, and there were some muffled acknowledgments.

"I've called you here because we're going to make another change. A change that will affect each one of you."

All eyes suddenly were focused on the president of the company. Thoughts of firings and layoffs arose.

"I've talked with all of you about the difference between leading and supervising. Your overwhelming responses have been that you want to lead, not supervise. You have also agreed that your titles should be changed. So as of today, if you agree, you're going to be called 'leads.' After all, as one of you pointed out, this term more closely describes the expectations of the individuals who will be orchestrating the actions of the employees."

Peter paused here to allow everyone to absorb what he had just said. "We are going to have a different form of supervision than we currently have, and it's going to be different than many traditional organizations. There will be no supervisors in the plant—each department will have a working lead person. Leads will learn how to become educators, facilitators, trainers, team coaches, and manufacturing engineers who will help other people grow as they—you, the leads—grow. But your job is going to change. Your role is going to change."

"Coaches? Engineers? We don't have any engineers here," snarled Tom, a large, barrel-chested supervisor.

"Not yet," Peter said calmly.

One of the supervisors asked, "Earlier you said we'd each be a coach and an educator?"

"Yes. That's right. We're going to try to remove the walls between workers and management. You'll learn new skills."

Another supervisor voiced a legitimate concern. "What if we can't learn this new way of managing?"

"I think everyone in this room is capable of learning. We will provide all the help and training you need. But you have to be willing to learn."

Someone then asked, "What if we can't accept this new way of managing?"

Peter was pained. "If you can't accept this new way of managing as a lead, and you can't accept any other position, then there may not be any room for you here at Magic. But, believe me, we will work with you or try to find another area for you. If that doesn't work, then we'll try to find you a job outside the company."

Ashley, a single mother of three and a supervisor in the wire department, was quite intrigued by what she was hearing. "I'm interested in this concept," she remarked. "Could you tell us more about leads?"

"Our leads will be the drivers of the policies," said Peter. "It's extremely important that this new leadership group—the leads—buy into an overall communication program, be trained properly, and be able to communicate. Because if we don't have the key leaders agreeing about what should be done, and communicating better, then we're missing out on a wealth of possibilities. And, we're stifling people from growing."

Tom, a press room supervisor, scoffed at the idea. But Ashley and another supervisor wanted to hear more.

Fred Ulrich looked at Peter and then took over the meeting. "All leads will attend weekly meetings with me. After the meetings, the leads will go back to their departments and hold weekly departmental meetings with everyone in their department. You may not think this is important, but I'll tell you—it is!"

"It sounds like a waste of time to me," said Tom.

"Well, Tom, if these meetings aren't conducted properly, they *will* be a waste of time."

Tom was becoming more indignant. "Look, I've been a foreman for a lot of years, both here and at other plants," he barked. "And I'm not about to kowtow to anyone, especially the workers. There is a chain of command, and I'm in that chain of command. But I always knew the buck stopped with us foremen. In any company, it's our butts that are on the line. And it's our job to kick butt and take names. So why do we need all of this nonsense?"

"We need it to survive and to grow," said Peter. "That's why all of you leads will go through extensive training on how to improve your leadership skills and your communication skills."

"I know how to communicate," said Tom as he roughly pushed his chair out and stood up. "There's no way I'm going to buy into this bunk. I say if you give a worker an inch, he'll take a mile. I've been here for four years, and maybe that was four years too long." He then walked out of the room and slammed the door.

"I'm sorry that Tom feels that way," Peter began. Everyone in the room knew that he was sincere. "I hope you understand that I am truly concerned about each and every one of you. I'm concerned about everyone here at Magic. I am not looking for ways to eliminate your jobs; I'm looking for ways to improve your jobs. To improve the culture here. To save the company. And it's not going to be easy. It's going to take everyone's cooperation. But the leads will play an important part in this company, and that's not to take away from the other people."

The supervisors seemed interested in the discussion. "Our goal is to have excellent up and down communication," explained Ulrich. "In most companies, communication usually goes only one way—and that's down. In other words, it goes from the top down to the supervisors, and from the supervisors down to the shop floor. But there is no movement going the other way, which tends to turn people off toward communication. This tells them that their opinions are not important. We want our communication to go both ways."

Ashley asked Ulrich to elaborate on the weekly meetings.

He explained that the two-way communication would be accomplished by having weekly lead meetings and departmental meetings. Ulrich would conduct the lead meetings, and the topics for the departmental meetings would come from the lead meetings. The leads would use the information and agenda from the lead meetings as a guideline for holding their departmental meetings.

Ulrich emphasized the importance of the workers' voices. He explained that the departmental meetings would include the ideas and comments of the workers from the various departments, and will become a part of the leads' agenda as well.

Ashley asked when the meetings would be held. Ulrich had not thought that far ahead and was open to suggestions.

"On the days when our departmental meetings are held we should have some overlap of the two shifts," said Ashley. "This will allow both shifts to get together, see one another, and form a little better communication among everyone in the entire department."

Peter, Keen, and Ulrich could not believe their ears. They definitely knew one supervisor who would become a lead. And their smiles told Ashley how they felt about her idea.

"Thank you for that suggestion," said Peter. "I think most of you are beginning to grasp what we're talking about here. The more communication channels we can open up between management and workers, workers and workers, departments and departments, and so on, the more improvement we'll begin to see. But it's going to start with us, every one of you in this room."

"And it's not an overnight type of thing," added Ulrich. "But I do believe that as soon as communication opens up among everyone throughout the plant, things will begin to change and improve."

Peter brought up an important point. "Another benefit of improved communication will be less wasted time and fewer misunderstandings. Remember when the wrong material was used on the Universal job, or when we put four hours into a setup only to find out it was the wrong machine, or when we had a pizza party and no one told shipping? All of these incidents were the result of some form of missed communication."

"We can sure use better communication," said Scott, the spring department supervisor. "Fifty percent of our scrap is the result of misunderstandings—or should I say, the result of miscommunication."

Ulrich continued to explain the weekly meeting concept. "The leads will conduct every one of their departmental meetings. When a lead isn't present, the meeting will be run by a second lead from the department."

One of the supervisors wanted to know if supervisors would be conducting these meetings by themselves. Ulrich explained that either he or Chet would sit in on all departmental meetings. "But," he emphasized, "we only do this to assist. For example, occasionally you may look to us for verification of a point brought up in a meeting. Or, you may need us to add some additional information to a topic being discussed. But we're not there to run the meetings; these are clearly your meetings."

"We want to make sure that the same message is consistently going out to all the departments," Peter added. "When we're holding eleven departmental meetings, we have to have a common denominator to make sure everyone is getting the same information."

He got a few nervous stares.

"Some of you may be thinking that you'll be afraid to hold meetings," said Peter. "Don't worry. We'll work with you on that. What we want to do is create an atmosphere on the shop floor for open communication and open-door policies. We want you to encourage people to speak at these meetings. And we want to develop enough trust so workers know that they'll get answers to their questions, which lets them know they're important. This can be referred to as *betterment, not bitterment.*"

A supervisor from the end of the table asked, "What if we don't give them the answer they want to hear?"

"The answer you give them may not always be what they want to hear, but their questions will always be answered and then we'll move on," replied Peter. "*We have to create an environment, though, where people trust each other so they can say things and openly talk things over.*" Ashley smiled, and he continued, "Once you get that out of the way, and people see that they don't get their head cut off for asking a question or making a suggestion, then the flow starts from there."

Peter closed the meeting with a profound statement. "You have to understand that all questions are important! Whether they are important to you at that time or not, they are important to the people asking them."

He took advantage of the opportunity to remind the group that the company's main focus would be on educating everyone regarding their work skills as well as nurturing their personal growth. He also discussed how groups would be created to identify Herbie issues.

"This will take some time," Peter admitted, "but our lines of communication will be direct and clear. At next week's meeting, we will review all of this, and I'll explain in more detail how the Herbie sessions will be conducted as well as review our own list of Herbies that we identified as a group—housekeeping, preventive maintenance, material problems, and reducing setup times."

9

Discovering the Weakest Link

"If One Is to Take a Thousand Year Journey, What Is the First Thing to Do?"

Peter had organized times for various groups to brainstorm with Keen. At these brainstorming meetings, the professor discussed the weakest link, explained the brainstorming rules, encouraged everyone to participate, and then facilitated the Herbie sessions. When Peter saw Keen he could not wait to ask the professor how things went. "What did you think of the brainstorming sessions?"

Keen hesitantly remarked that the workers had some pent-up frustrations. "Their perceptions about Magic are a lot different from mine."

"I'm interested in learning what you have discovered." Keen reminded Peter that the two of them, as well as Fred Ulrich, had copies of all the Herbies. And they would soon be getting together with Chet for a full day or two to discuss them. The professor added that he wanted to wait until the four of them could all share their perceptions about these before he formed an opinion on any of the Herbies.

A week later, the professor and Peter walked into the conference room and sat down with Fred and Chet to discuss the items listed by the workers as possible Herbies. Each group had been asked, "If you could change things at Magic to strengthen its weakest links, what would they be?" Then each group had picked out its top two Herbies.

One item on several lists was pay. So Peter asked, "Do you think if we doubled their pay they would double the output and profits?"

"No way," Chet quickly responded.

Peter assured them that it was rather common for workers to assume that they were underpaid. "We have to look beyond the money issue to see what we can do to really change the company so we can increase the wages here, or would their efficiency increase 150%? No way!"

Then Peter, John, Chet and Fred went through every one of the more than three hundred Herbies—discussing, challenging, debating, and arguing. Keen asked them what they were learning from this process and what their insights were.

"Well, we certainly have a lot of people with the wrong impression of what is trying to be accomplished at Magic," Peter remarked.

Fred commented that he could not believe some of the things that had been said.

Chet was just shaking his head.

"What about you, Chet," Keen asked.

"I just can't believe this is happening at Magic."

Keen stood up. "But look at the opportunity we now have," he said, while using his hands to emphasize each word.

Peter leaned forward. "The next step is for me, and whichever of you can make the meetings, to go back to each group and review each of the Herbies with them one by one.

"This will help us clear up many of the wrong impressions that workers have and show them that we are sincere about listening to their ideas. It will also help us to more fully understand some of these Herbie statements and give us a chance to have a dialogue on any other issues that might be bothering them at this time. It will improve communications."

Keen was pleased with the direction of this meeting. He asked if there was any other way that Magic might benefit by having these communication sessions.

"I think the workers will learn more about what's on other people's minds as well as what management is thinking," said Chet.

"Anything else?"

Peter, in his teasing manner, said, "Give us a clue."

"I don't want to weaken my story," Keen replied. "That's your clue."

"Some clue," joked Ulrich.

Peter scratched his chin. "We're back to the weak link again?"

"Yes. What about the weak link?"

"Okay, then. If we only focus on our weak links, then we can all communicate more clearly because we all know what has to be done to improve."

"Beautiful," the professor enthusiastically responded as he took his seat. "It's easier to communicate policies, perform operations, and have everyone pulling the same way for the betterment of Magic."

Peter stood up and walked to the overhead transparency projector. "After hearing from employees and management, it looks like we have five areas to focus on for major improvements—preventive maintenance, setup times, housekeeping, material problems, and a sample board of parts so that the shipping and setup people will know exactly what the parts should look like. What do the rest of you think?"

Chet asked, "What about education and training?"

Peter replied, "You're correct. That is our weakest link."

"That's the way we read it, too," said Chet and Fred.

Peter turned to Keen. "Professor, what do you think?"

"I think that Chet is correct. We have selected some major bottlenecks, but not our constraint. A constraint is the bottleneck that holds one back the most, relative to achieving one's goal."

Everyone was wondering what the professor was talking about now?

Keen continued, "The five bottlenecks have one thing in common. Anyone know what it is?"

Fred said, "All five major improvement areas identified slow down our ability to get our parts to our customers."

"Well said, Fred," replied Keen.

"However, what is common about these five improvement areas?" repeated the professor.

Peter said, "Every one of the five opportunities that we have identified would be improved if the proper education and training were given to our associates. Education is really our constraint; the bottleneck that holds us back the most."

"Peter, it can't be said any better than that," responded Keen.

Peter said, "we need to establish an educational and training program that is second to none. What if we called it Life Long Education?"

Everyone at the table said, "Great idea!"

Keen, in one of his many ways of making a point, asked a question by using a Chinese proverb. "*If one is to take a thousand-year journey, what is the first thing one must do?*"

"*Take that first step,*" said Chet.

"Good answer," Peter said. "So why don't we take the first step and call it a day?"

"Sounds good to me," Keen agreed. "But don't forget to share with the workers not only what we are going to focus on but how we are going to do it."

10

Quality of Life Issues

"What Gets Measured Gets Done"

Winds were swirling in pathways that only the spirits could follow, and the trees were at their color peak for the fall season when Keen arrived at Magic on Monday for his Herbie strategy session with Peter. It did not seem possible that over two years had passed since Keen met Peter.

"Happy new day," Keen said as he entered Peter's office.

"Same to you," Peter replied. "You are here to brainstorm about how to present the Herbie results. Right?"

"Yes I am. And I'm looking forward to it."

"We need to review the overall strategy of how the results for our Herbie meeting today might be presented to everyone in the plant," suggested Peter.

"You're the owner and CEO of this company because of your many talents and abilities. Beyond that, however, you also know to use empathy when presenting and listening to the comments that will be made about the Herbies and what you're planning to do with them."

"Empathy is an empowerment concept," Peter said, half jokingly.

"It is. And that's an area we need to discuss and implement at a later date. For right now, though, why don't we have a go at how you're going to approach your sessions."

"Okay," said Peter as he removed his sport coat. "I'll sit down with each group and discuss their Herbies one by one."

"How? Do you have a plan?"

Peter thought for a moment. "With an open mind and patience."

"Good."

"Also, I'll explain the correct Magic perspective on the issues and promise only what we can do. I'll also share that we are establishing focus groups to concentrate on the areas that they decided needed changing the most."

In anticipation of this response, Keen had prepared a small poster that listed all of the focus groups. He slipped the poster out of his briefcase and held it up to show Peter, who just laughed. Peter knew what Keen was doing. The professor was saying that unless everyone is reminded over and over they will quickly forget what they have heard or seen.

Peter had already appreciated, as had many of the management team, that they had to have more practice in coaching and teaching people over and over. Just as an athlete must practice to get better at executing the fundamentals, the management team needed to practice in order to improve in their roles. Magic was learning new fundamentals everyday about how to compete better in the global market.

The professor also shared other important learning tools. He had explained in some of the management learning sessions that visual aids should supplement verbal information, and vice versa, because the more senses that one uses in learning, the higher the retention rate of that learning.

"John, I agree with your comments, but we need to somehow relate this to our focus areas of housekeeping, preventive maintenance, sample board, materials and setup time reduction."

"Any ideas?" asked Keen.

"I've been thinking about our education and training constraint as well as the other five bottlenecks," Peter replied.

"I believe that, since setup time reduction requires more time to achieve, we should single this one bottleneck out more than the other four. What if we called it our 4+1 improvement program?" continued Peter.

"I like the concept of 4+1." Keen held up four fingers on one hand and the index finger on the other. "We can use our fingers for communicating to our focus groups the five areas that we are going to focus on."

Peter continued. "Furthermore, I'll share with everyone that we are in the process of choosing individuals for the different focus groups, and that we'll have a mix of people in each focus group in order to take advantage of any cross-functional issues. Hopefully, by doing this we'll synchronize the flow of work throughout the company."

"How are you going to choose people for these focus groups?"

"Anyone who is interested in being considered for such a group should tell one of the leads, Chet, Fred, or me," explained Peter. "And they should let us know as soon as possible. I'll also tell them that we will select the leader of each group, provide him or her with a starting mission statement, and post the membership in about two weeks."

"Do you think that's how housekeeping, safety, and preventive maintenance impacts everyone's quality of life should be discussed?" Keen inquired.

"Yes. I believe spending time explaining the significance of these items as related to how they improve their quality of life is important."

Peter agreed and said he would be glad to do that. He then asked if there was anything else.

"What's your feeling about safety?"

"There is no choice when it comes to safety," said Peter. "You know how I feel, given all the programs and concerns we have for our people." Involved in manufacturing his entire adult life, Peter knew that a strong safety program was appreciated by everyone in the company. "Safety has to be a dominant factor. We must always strive to make everyone and everything here as safe as humanly possible. We must care about our internal customers first, before we can take care of our external customers. When it comes to spending time and money, safety and quality come first. Why do you ask?"

"What are you going to do about it?"

"What do you mean?"

"Well, as you know, *what gets measured gets done!*"

"Okay. What are you thinking?"

"You already have a small poster by the time clock that indicates the number of days since the last time anyone at Magic lost a day of work because of an accident. Right? What are you doing every day to make the place safer?"

"We have a task force that meets once a month to see what is happening."

"You said task force."

"Whoops! I forgot. I meant to say focus group."

When Magic initially began organizing groups, they were referred to as task forces. But a task force (sometimes thought of as a hard word) does its job and is then discontinued. However, a focus group (a soft word) is like a flashlight that is always shining and focusing on where you want to go. By using focus groups, Magic would continually illuminate the areas where they wanted to focus their attention.

"Right on," said Keen. He had just heard evidence that his over and over and over theory works. "Well, you already have a safety committee, and you have safety buttons, and you investigate all accidents. But I have an idea I would like you to consider."

"What is it?"

"Place a large white board in the best strategic place for workers to see and use. Invite anyone at any time to write down any safety idea. We should also communicate that anyone can personally give the safety committee their idea. Some workers are reluctant to write things down because of spelling and difficulty in writing. The more flexibility we use in getting ideas, the better."

The two men were quiet for a moment. Then Peter began, "I want this place to be safe for everyone. I do care about everyone. Our associates are our most important asset, and I mean it. Not like the company I used to work for that said the same but acted differently. I used to get signature-stamped Christmas cards from the chairman."

"That also reminds me of some management teams that say they have participative management, associates, teammates, or what have you, and then you see the office staff or suits having free coffee while the rest have to bring or buy their coffee. In the parking lot we see designated parking spaces. When it snows, who gets their parking area plowed first? The office workers have private bathrooms while the rest use a general one. Over-the-counter medicine such as aspirins and the like are kept under lock and key, and the hourly employees have to request them, while the office people just walk in and help themselves. Workers are held to a rigid timetable of arrival and departure, while the office workers come and go at various times. Do the office personnel punch in and out of work?"

Keen was nodding in agreement. He had seen all of this and more.

Peter continued. "It's interesting to me to see managers claim one thing and then act the other way with some rationale to justify it. Who are they kidding? It certainly isn't their workers. I don't believe this is the way to grow people or a team."

The professor then suggested that Magic should keep an accurate history of all safety changes and the dollars spent. Current and future workers should be made aware of these accomplishments from time to time. "I believe in recording Magic's tribal history, so that everyone can take pride and ownership in what has been achieved," Keen explained.

"You're big on this tribal history stuff. Do you honestly believe there's value in it?"

"I certainly do! For instance, the number of safety ideas generated and the implemented responses are how we'll measure the quality of life issue for safety. You've been keeping a tribal history at Magic without even realizing it."

"You mean the collages?"

"Yes," said Keen. "Your collages are part of the tribal history here. They provide recognition. They're a self-esteem builder. A pride factor."

Peter thought about his collages, which had come about quite by accident. When he had first bought the company, he had had a roll of film he wanted to get developed. He had taken ten of the twenty-four pictures at home and was anxious to get the photos back. To use up the remaining pictures on the roll, he had gone out onto the shop floor and snapped some pictures of the workers. He had posted all of the photographs on the bulletin board, and it had become an instant hit with everyone. When he was taking the pictures, a few people had not wanted their picture taken. But when the photos were put on display, they had all run up to the information board to see if their picture was there.

Over the two years, Peter began taking more and more pictures. Then, at the end of each year, he made a collage and hung it on the wall near the lunchroom. In the center of the collage was the year and a few key words to describe the most significant change made at Magic for that period, surrounded by nearly seventy-five photographs. Since that first time more than two years ago, Peter had made several collages each year. The last collage had contained over three hundred pictures. Everyone appeared at least once in each collage. Furthermore, looking at the collages had become a conversation piece and a marketing tool for the many visitors who came to talk to the Magic people.

"How are we going to measure the quality of life issues for housekeeping and preventive maintenance?" he asked Keen.

"Well, let's first give the focus groups a chance. It'll be better if they invent the answers. The buy-in is more assured that way. Of course, at times we might raise questions in a Socratic manner. Now, how many quality of life issues for helping to grow people have we identified so far?"

"Well, my absentminded friend, if my memory serves me correctly, we have three: housekeeping, preventive maintenance, and safety. Are there any others?"

"Yes, I'm sure there are. However, Rome wasn't built in a day. Let's just make sure that our first Herbie response to the workers does not overwhelm them."

"Back to the topic of the meetings," said Peter. "At first, I'll be discussing these issues with the leads. After I get their input, I will arrange to meet with the other groups."

"What do you think might happen if you did not share your findings and plans with the leads first?"

Peter thought for a moment. "They would not be very happy with me, and they wouldn't buy in as much if we bypassed them. Also, I'd be missing out on their input about how to better present the information. One or more of them might provide me with better insights than I think I have now. But, to tell you the truth, I've always tried to bounce things off my management first."

"What do you think might happen with the 4+1 focus and the quality of life issues if the managers weren't involved first? What might happen if some of the more assertive workers got all fired up and wanted to implement all kinds of positive ideas related to these 4+1 areas that we are focusing on at this time?"

"I hope they do. What's your point?"

"All leads are not created equal," said Keen. "When they have their departmental meetings, someone might present an idea that is right on the mark. How might a weak lead react to such an idea?"

"Maybe he'd suppress it because he'd feel that he should have thought of it," said Peter. "We need to educate and encourage our leads to understand that this might happen to them. And that it's okay. At Magic we don't really care who comes up with the idea."

"What do you think might happen if the workers had a problem and couldn't solve it?" asked Keen.

"Our leads would help them?"

"What might happen if neither one knew how to solve the problem?"

Peter closed his eyes while he thought about how he might answer. "Oh, you mean problem-solving techniques."

"Yes. There are many problem-solving methods to choose from. However, the one selected should be standardized for everyone at Magic. *Standardization makes workers' expectations more clear as well as fosters clearer communication on the same things.*"

"We need to educate all our workers on problem-solving techniques if we want better results," Peter said. "That's just good common sense. We need to sort this out and plan to incorporate it into our education sessions."

"What might have been the results of the forthcoming focus groups after they had picked the low-fruit problems?" inquired Keen.

"What do you mean?"

"Focus groups can usually solve easy problems but don't know how to solve complex problems," said Keen.

Peter paused for a moment. Then he remarked, "Somehow they'll have to learn how to climb higher in the tree to get the rest of the fruit."

"Yes. But how can they do that if they don't have the tools? And what if they don't know how to climb?" asked Keen.

"They don't get any more fruit. Magic needs to provide the tools so that the workers are willing and able to climb higher to get all the fruit that the tree has to offer us."

"I couldn't have said it better," the professor said jokingly. "Does problem solving fit in with any other of our ideas for Magic?"

"Well, I guess that when everyone gets accustomed to using problem solving and sees the results, they will feel good about it." Peter pointed his finger at Keen as if to say 'gotcha.' "I know where you're heading. Their self-esteem and the growing of people thing. Is this another quality of life issue?"

"As usual, you have invented the answer."

"I never fully realized until we started sharing ideas that without problem-solving tools, we're limited as to the actual problems we can solve— much less identify."

"That's right. So let's be sure to share these concepts with the leads when you meet with them. And remember, the more times they hear it the better. It starts to become a part of their beliefs and behavior. As you stated earlier, the leads need to know first before their departments do."

Peter and Keen were exhausted, but pleased. They always enjoyed these 1,001 question sessions.

Keen asked if he could sit in on a few of the Herbie feedback sessions. He wanted to get a feeling for what was happening and to see the workers' reactions to the dialogue.

"That'll be fine," said Peter. "You know that you're always welcome."

11

Eliminate Waste

*"Require Workers to Put Their Brains Into Action
Instead of Leaving Them at the Door"*

The first several Herbie meetings with the workers went extremely well. One by one Peter dispelled the perceptions that were not on target, and people fleshed out the concerns that he did not fully understand. These meetings gave Peter a chance to interact with the workers and to share his vision with them. They also gave him the opportunity to discuss what direction Magic was going to focus on and how everyone was going to approach the various problems.

"One thing that became evident from studying your lists of concerns during the past several weeks is that many of us do not know the overall focus of our company or the practical work involved in the overall process here at Magic. This includes leads, toolmakers, salespeople, shipping, receiving, and everyone. Even me. Most of us are involved in only our own operation, and we have no idea as to the role it plays in the overall scheme of things here."

Peter stood up. "An important goal for each of us is to get to know the operations here from top to bottom. One of the most difficult aspects of manufacturing is understanding the complexity of each operation and its effects on the others. The process between entering orders and shipping them can be very convoluted."

"We receive an order and the materials arrive at our plant," he said. "We then implement the process. And at the conclusion of the process, we ship the products to our customers. This much is cut and dried. Each of us knows our job and what we're supposed to do, but we're not aware of what else takes place during the entire operation—from beginning to completion. In other words, who does what, when, where, how, and why."

Keen was sitting in on this meeting and just could not keep his mouth closed. "World-class companies synchronize the flow of work through their system," he said. "This is sometimes known as 'synchronization,' which is a big word that means we understand the importance of everyone's job and how we are all dependent on each other."

Peter appreciated Keen's comments. Someone in the group spoke up and asked the question that was on everyone's mind. "How are we going to do this synchronization stuff? Do you have some plan?"

"Yes, we do," said Peter. "And you'll be learning about this and more in our meetings. But first, we must break down the organizational barriers that exist and understand what really goes on in the overall process here. I suppose there are two versions to this statement. Some people have worked in a company for ten years and have never been in the southwest corner of the building in which they work. They have no clue or direction as to what's going on there. That's one version. Another version is that management, as a team, does not really understand the full process flow from the time an order is received until the order is shipped. They don't understand how it goes through the plant."

A few snickers emanated from the group. "My money's on the second version," someone jokingly said.

"Yeah, especially the sales department," a worker chided.

"You may very well be right," said Peter. "But from this day on, everyone in this company is going to know the entire operation." Peter stood up and passed out copies of the forms. The directions were listed as:

Whenever possible, follow an actual task in progress.
Write down each step—including transport, waiting, delay, storage.
Record elapsed time and/or distance traveled.
Color in the circle to indicate value-added steps (see form).
Make the following calculations: (# VA steps/# steps), (VA time/total time), and (distance)

"Now, I want to show you what can be revealed by completing a Process-Analysis Form," Peter said, as he placed a transparency on the overhead projector. Then he asked everyone to take a typical example of wire or flat stock used at Magic and list all the processing steps it goes through. They came up with a total of twenty steps. Next he asked them to consider the time and distance a part traveled.

"Waste can be defined as anything that does not add value for our customers. This can include how people, materials, and machines spend time—or, in many instances, waste time.

"Number one is the people. People spend time waiting for materials to work on, watching machines running, producing defects, looking for tools, fixing machine breakdowns, producing unnecessary items, accumulating inventories, performing rework, contending with a shortage of parts, paper systems, dealing with rules, and working on unnecessary office tasks.

"Number two is the materials. Materials spend time in transportation, storage, inspection, and rework.

"Number three is the machines. Machines contribute to waste by unnecessary movement of the machine, setup time, machine breakdown, unproductive maintenance, production of defective and unneeded products, and idle time.

"Out of the twenty steps that wire or flat stock goes through in our plant, which ones add value?"

The group was hesitant about answering. "Remember, value added usually means a change to the part that the customer is willing to pay for," Peter reminded them.

After twenty minutes, they could only agree on two steps that added value.

"So that means there are eighteen steps that do not add value," Peter pointed out. "The companies that can eliminate as many of these unneeded steps—or non-value added steps—as possible are going to survive in the twenty-first century. There's no way you can really eliminate them all, but your goal is to keep trying."

"It's seems so simple," a shipping department employee commented. "If you've got eighteen unneeded steps, then you eliminate the eighteen steps."

"That just about sums it up," said Peter. "However, you probably will never completely eliminate all eighteen wasted steps, but the companies that keep trying will be the survivors. Also, you can't entirely eliminate all of the paperwork."

"So, what are some of your ideas?" Peter asked. "Think of the difference between the way conditions are now and the way they could be or should be. How can we eliminate the wasted steps?"

Phil from the four-slide department suggested, "Maybe we could work with our suppliers so they can learn and grow with us."

Another member of the group said, "What if when inventory comes in we put it right by the machine rather than moving it around a lot."

"Good idea," praised Peter, pleased with the positive thinking of his associates.

Doug from the spring department said, "Maybe we could package some of our parts at the machines. On the one hand, this may mean a lot more work for us. But on the other hand, it could save us a lot of time in the shipping department."

"We could even do the bar-coding at the machine," someone interjected.

"Excellent!" Peter said. "And, believe it or not, it may not mean that much extra work for anybody. Also, as costs go down due to improved quality and delivery we will get more business, which means secured jobs, better pay and benefits, and improved working conditions."

Peter was ecstatic at the ideas he was hearing.

"The tool we have been working on in engineering could eliminate a lot of waste," an older machinist stated.

"You mean the Smart Tool?" Peter asked.

"Yes."

Most of the group seemed confused. So, Peter decided it was a good time to reveal Magic's newest and most sophisticated idea for adding value and eliminating waste for the customer. "Some of you may not be aware that we have a tool that we've been working on for two years. Our nickname for it is Smart Tool."

Peter pushed his chair out and stood up. "Our vision for this type of tooling is to have stamping dies that will run at high speed, automatically adjusting for critical dimensions while the machine is running, and give full SPC data."

Some mouths were hanging open in disbelief. "Wow," was the overwhelming reaction. "How fast can we get these Smart Tools?"

"It'll be years," Peter admitted. "It's still in development. But we currently have high hopes and one working tool. Hopefully, we'll be able to apply the techniques to other tools in the near future. Several people have put in a lot of time and effort into this project," Peter said. "I'd like to thank you. Does everyone realize what we've accomplished?"

People were smiling, but no one volunteered an answer.

"We've put forth an effort to eliminate waste," Peter said. "And these efforts are going to pay off in a big way. A real big way. But these efforts can't stop when you go out onto the shop floor. If you think something can be done better, faster, safer, or easier, give it a try. Another example, but a different process, is why we eliminated time clocks. The primary reason we did this may have been to build trust, but we also did it because the time-keeper did not add value."

After everyone had left the meeting, Keen walked over to Peter. "This was a powerful meeting. You have required the workers to put their brains into action instead of leaving them at the door like a lot of companies do."

"Thank you," said Peter. "I've always believed that if you treat the people in your department like jackasses, they'll acquire all the attributes of that unruly animal. But treat them as intelligent adult human beings, and they'll fulfill that expectation. So I'm going to expect a lot from these people, and I have the feeling they're going to surpass my expectations."

"If today's meeting is any indication of what you can expect from them, I have to agree with you," said Keen. "And you really have used the Pygmalion Theory."

"What are you talking about now?"

"The Pygmalion Theory is the idea that if a person is given an expectation, it becomes reality to that person. Doctors have used this throughout time to help patients heal themselves. Doctors would tell patients that this or that would cure them, and the patients would start programming themselves to be in a healthy state of existence again. The point is that expectations are like psychological affirmations."

"You can put a name to anything, professor," Peter said, shaking his head.

12

Trust, Relationships, Integrity, and Communication

"Use Key Words and Phrases to
Improve Communications"

Peter had finished the time-consuming task of meeting over the last two weeks with everyone in the plant in the follow-up Herbie meetings. He felt as if he were learning things every day. The whole picture was becoming clearer. Still, he thought, what good is having the big picture if I am the only one who can see it? He had to begin synthesizing for a broader group the key perceptions that the workers had shared. He would begin with the leads. He thought that since most people at Magic perceived things to be the way they had shared with him, it was probably reality for them, and the leads should know it.

He walked in on Chet, Fred, and Keen having coffee at the plant. Chet was complaining as Peter walked up. "I hate introducing change. Especially when we ask workers for weaknesses. They expect everything will be changed just like they want," he said snapping his fingers.

"You'll go through a bitching and moaning period," Peter explained, "but as you read between the lines, you'll start to see that there are some kernels of truth in the things they are saying. We have to focus on the Herbies, or I should say, the 4+1 program. As we start to do this and changes are made, people will begin to buy in more and more as they see the changes implemented."

"But aren't most leads afraid of bitching and moaning?" Fred asked.

"Most managers are afraid to stand up in front of people and have them bitch and moan at them," Peter agreed. "So we'll have to teach the leads some skills for how to handle discipline and other situations. Any suggestions?"

Keen made a suggestion. "Well, I think if you're honest and take the sting out of the stinger, the bitching and moaning won't be that bad."

"I also believe there will be less bitching and moaning if people understand *why* something has to be done," said Peter. "They may or may not like the change at first, but if they understand what's happening to cause it or what will happen if it isn't implemented, they usually have little difficulty in adjusting. But first, managers and leads need to completely internalize why something has to be done, and they have to be able to explain the why to people. Furthermore, we need to spend some time discussing discipline and criticism in the future."

Chet and Fred headed back to work. Peter walked toward his office to answer a phone call, and Keen decided to take a stroll through the plant. As he walked through the wire department, Ashley motioned to him. Approaching her, he asked, "How are you today?"

"I'm fine. But I didn't sleep much last night. I came up with an idea that was so exciting I couldn't wait to get here to tell you and Peter." The excitement in her voice was overwhelming. Keen could not believe it. He also could not believe that leads and workers were thinking of ways to improve their jobs and the company on their own time.

"I've noticed the atmosphere changing here," Ashley continued. "It's changed quite a bit. And the change has definitely been for the better. But there is still something missing. We all know what it is. It's so obvious. But we haven't been able to pinpoint it. There is one more 'environment factor' that we need to institute into everything we do here."

"What is it?" asked Keen.

Ashley smiled and then confidently stated, "Trust. We need to build up the trust." She paused to allow her statement to sink in, then added, "And we've got to continue to remove walls, such as the traditional salaried/hourly mind-set."

Keen instantly agreed with her, and he was barely able to contain his excitement. He felt like doing cartwheels down the center of the aisle, even though he had never done a cartwheel before in his life. The professor knew that Ashley had found a significant piece of the puzzle. He immediately realized that trust was also probably the linchpin that would affect all the changes that would take place at the company. He grabbed Ashley's hand and they practically sprinted together down to Peter's office.

"Ashley found the missing ingredient to everything we are doing here," Keen said as they burst into Peter's office. "She found the key—she found the linchpin—she—"

"OK, OK. I get the picture," Peter said. "But what are you talking about?"

"Trust," Ashley said.

Keen burst in. "Ashley thought of this last night, on her own time, at home. I know we've touched upon the subject of trust and breaking down the barriers, but we've never really emphasized it. And for some reason, the way that Ashley put it caused me to see the entire issue in the proper perspective for the first time."

Peter looked at Ashley and smiled. "I commend you. I've been thinking along similar lines. Not about trust, though. I've been thinking about relationships here. Along with relationships, I've given a lot of thought to integrity and communication. And trust fits into that perfectly," Peter said, interlocking his fingers together to show how trust, relationships, integrity, and communication fit together. "In fact, now that you've brought it up, trust may be the most vital part of the four areas."

Keen joined in. "I guess I've been in sync with the two of you for some time now, too, even though we've never shared our thoughts on this topic. But I've always said that every breath that we take in our lives—our personal lives, our professional lives, our spiritual lives, and our social lives—from the cradle to the grave, is spent in either 'P' squared or 'S' squared. P^2 is personal and professional. S^2 is spiritual and social. Whatever you do, it's going to fall into one of those four areas. And trust, relationships, integrity, and communication should be the foundation for all four of those areas of our lives, because if there's darkness in one department of your life, there are shadows in the other parts. If there's brightness in one, there's sunshine in the other ones as well. And trust, relationships, integrity, and communication help you to get that brightness. If you don't use them, there's darkness."

Ashley added, "We can teach people to speak up, to be honest, to help people grow with each other. I also believe that we should practice soft words with the foundation of trust, relationships, integrity and communication." Ashley turned her notebook around to show Peter and Keen.

> **T**rust
> **R**elationships
> **I**ntegrity
> **C**ommunication

They stopped talking and looked at her tablet with quizzical expressions on their faces. "T.R.I.C.," she said, drawing their attention to the first letter of each word. "TRIC! One word says it all."

Keen and Peter loved the acronym.

"TRIC," Peter repeated. "A magic trick." After saying it, he burst out laughing. "Get it? Magic trick. This is the magic. But it's going to take a long time. And it can be fragile."

"It will take some time, but I think it's wonderful," Keen rejoiced. "Because you've got to have some basic values that you believe in, and that's where trust, relationships, integrity, and—excuse me, that's where 'TRIC' comes in. Treating people like you want to be treated."

"I agree. But trust is not going to develop overnight," Peter cautioned. "We're going to have to start slowly. It's something that's going to have to develop and take root. Maybe in the beginning, we can use TRIC as sort of a crutch to help people to open up a little more with each other."

"Maybe we can call TRIC the Quality of Trust, Relationships, Integrity, & Communication," said Ashley. Peter and Keen looked at her with huge smiles. "I'm going to TRIC you," she laughed. "Maybe people can say, 'I'm going to approach you with TRIC,'" she continued. "And this can mean that they're going to discuss some issue that they may not be too comfortable with, so be a little more loving toward each other."

"As of this moment, we will incorporate TRIC into our culture," said Peter. The excitement in the room was infectious.

"Smashing!" said the professor.

"In fact, we need to establish a common vernacular for a lot more than just TRIC here at Magic," Peter continued. "This new language can be a part of our culture. What we need to do is take all of the key words and phrases that we've been using—words that are not just symbolism but have substance—and put them into terms so that everyone can talk to each other and know exactly what's being communicated. TRIC is a perfect example. Whenever that word is used we want everyone to know exactly what we mean. We need to also take words like quality, JIT, and others that we are now using and educate everyone as to their exact meanings."

"So everybody's singing the same hymn out of the same hymnbook," Ashley interjected.

Keen pointed out, "With everyone talking the same language, they'll be able to communicate Magic's goals and priorities more effectively. And this will help them to not only perform their jobs better, but also take more of an interest in what they're doing."

Peter finished the thought by adding, "We'll all be moving in the same direction toward our vision of being the best at what we do."

13

Energy Vampires

*"Many Westerners Want to Look Back and Talk
About How Far They Have Come, Instead of How Far
They Have to Go"*

Today's meeting of the leads was the largest one yet. Besides all of the leads, Peter had asked one or two additional people from each department to participate. These additional people did not know it yet, but they were candidates for the position of second leads. Peter, Fred, and Chet had been observing everyone for the past few weeks, and they had selected these candidates for their leadership potential.

Keen was going to conduct this session and he jumped right into it. "What is a bad apple?"

"Yeah, one bad apple can spoil the whole bushel," said Phil, a bright, hardworking young man from the spring department.

"Negativity is like poison, it can kill or ruin healthy lives and a healthy environment. And it can destroy an organization." Then Keen paused before asking, "Do you have any bad apples here at Magic?"

A few people were shaking their heads. The general consensus of the group was that Magic was void of any bad apples.

"Is there someone here at Magic that if they didn't come to work tomorrow you feel you'd be happier and the company would be better off?"

Everyone's eyes were closed and Keen began to see smiles and grins throughout the group. Then someone asked, "Only one name? Can we do two?"

The professor turned to the projector and wrote on an overhead transparency 'definition of a bad apple.'

"They have a bad attitude," said Ashley. "They find fault in everything. And they're negative about most things and most people."

Phil claimed to know a couple of bad apples. And he said they had two things in common. Their vocabulary was in need of cleansing, and they seldom appeared to be happy.

"They're not willing to try, and they're not cooperative," said Scott.

Keen was busy writing down the definitions. "Can you think of any more? Come on, come on."

"They make everyone miserable," said Courtney, from the shipping department. "They just don't care. They don't care at all."

Scott came up with some more definitions: "Every mistake is always someone else's fault. They like to point a finger."

"Good," said Keen.

"High absenteeism," someone said. Then someone else asked, "Is that so bad? I always feel better when he doesn't show up." This comment brought some laughter. Even Peter was smiling. Then he reminded everyone that if a bad apple is always absent, others have to pick up his slack.

"I've got a definition," said Fred Ulrich. "They always talk about how it used to be done and why this new way is not as good."

The room got quiet. A lot of this kind of talk had been going around lately. But it seemed to be subsiding as more and more people were buying into the new concepts.

"I've also got a couple of attributes of a bad apple," said Peter. "They're not teachable. They're not supportive. And they're always second-guessing."

Keen finished writing the list, which was quite lengthy, and turned to the group. "In the same way that JIT encourages us to eliminate waste, we should also eliminate bad apples, because they do not add the type of value to the company we want. What does toxicity from a rattlesnake's bite do to one's body?" asked Keen.

Puzzled by the question, no one answered for a few moments. Finally Ashley replied, "It makes you sick and may even kill you."

"That's right. And the same principle applies to bad apples. They are toxic to our culture, and we need to clean them out like we purge poison from our body. We all want good health."

Keen continued. "Toxic people are the ones who always dwell on the negative. The dictionary defines toxic as 'poisonous.' And toxic people continually spew their verbal poison.

"After listening to toxic people, you can't help but feel depressed, drained, and listless. We can certainly call them 'bad apples,' but they could just as well be identified as *energy vampires* or *dream killers*. Is this the type of individual we want working at Magic? Is this the culture we want?"

The room resounded with a loud "no."

"Who controls your thoughts?" Keen asked.

Some of the people in the group seemed ready to answer immediately, but hesitated. Others looked around the room. After a few seconds, several said, "We do."

"You can control them to be positive or negative, to be constructive or destructive, to be happy or sad, to confront problems (bad apples) or let them slide. The choice is yours. What do you want to do about 'energy vampires?'"

"Throw them out!" someone yelled. Other responses were, "Put them in the dumpster," and "Get rid of them!" A final suggestion was, "Drive a stake through their heart."

The atmosphere was fired up with laughter.

"Is there anything else we could try to do with them before we follow your suggestions?" asked Keen.

There were a few moments of silence. Then Ashley spoke up, "Should we try and help them change their behavior?"

Sam from the stamping department scoffed. "That's wasting your time," he stated. "They will never change. I have worked with too many of them for too long a time."

"Are we able to unlearn habits?" Keen asked. "Or have our parents' genes programmed us to a lifetime of following their habits?"

"We can learn new habits," said Fred. "The question, as I see it, though, is whether or not we are willing to make a commitment to changing these dream killers. How are we going to sustain our continuous improvement journey if we are constantly spending our energy dealing with counterproductive behavior? We must learn to accept and even embrace change as the daily norm. Let's be honest with each other and promise that we'll work diligently to change the bad habits of a few people."

"Excellent insight," responded Keen. "How do you feel when you're around people who are upbeat, positive, enthusiastic, supportive, and constructive?"

Smiles filled the room. A few responses were, "refreshed and nourished," "can't get enough of them," and "the good life."

"I bet you would be encouraged and inspired," Keen said. "Also, as you share more time with nourishing people, your self-esteem grows. As it grows, so grows your willingness to make change. The more change that you can handle, the easier it is for you to cope with most everything. To the extent that you cope with most everything, your world of actions and expectations increases to the point that miracles seem to happen to you all the time.

"So we have to learn to take control of how we deal with people and our life," Keen explained. "We have to confront the bad apples, and as Ashley implied, we must give them a chance to change. If an individual doesn't change after a reasonable amount of coaching, then for their own good and that of the others at Magic, this bad apple worker should be employed somewhere else."

Keen stopped to take a sip of water. He then asked, "Is it fair to the other workers at Magic if one dream killer is allowed to spoil the culture we all want to live and work in everyday?"

Because the motivational beat of the meeting was ascending to its zenith by this time, the mountainous chorus of "no" could be heard outside the learning center.

Keen's voice became louder, more forceful. "Who has the authority, control, and responsibility for establishing and maintaining the culture at Magic?"

"We do!" came the booming reply.

"Then let's do it," Keen said as he raised his clenched fists in the air over his head in a gesture of victory. "We only limit ourselves. We can learn to coach, to manage, to lead, and to grow people. Thank you, Peter, for giving us the opportunity and encouragement to make changes."

Applause broke out in the room.

Peter decided that now (after the five-minute break) was a good time to talk to the group about leadership.

"The greatest responsibility of a leader is to lead people to growth," he said. "In other words, you need to grow people. Some of you may have heard the professor use that term. Well, you're going to be hearing that term a lot around here. I know that we've given you quite a bit of information to assimilate and consider, but Fred, Chet, and I have confidence in each and every one of you. We truly believe you are the future of Magic Manufacturing."

The faces in the room revealed a mixture of expressions. Some seemed doubtful, others self-confident, and still others confused. But a sense of pride could be seen on most of the faces.

After Peter finished, Keen picked up a handmade poster and placed it on the easel. "And now that we know what a bad apple is and what its attributes are, let's see what makes a good leader."

CHARACTERISTICS AND TRAITS OF A FUTURE LEADER AT MAGIC.

Has consistent and dependable integrity.
Is open to contrary opinion.
Communicates easily at all levels.
Understands the concept of equity and consistently advocates it.
Leads through serving.
Is vulnerable to the skills and talents of others.
Is intimate with the organization and its work.
Is able to see the broad picture (beyond one's own area of focus).
Is a spokesperson and diplomat.
Can be a tribal storyteller (an important way of transmitting corporate culture).
Leads with 'why' instead of 'what' to do.
Manages people instead of things.

"These are some of the things the leaders at Magic should be learning, and eventually doing. Some of you already possess many of these traits. Please be open-minded about all of this. And since you know the traits of both a bad apple and a leader, you've got to accentuate the positive and eliminate the negative." He put up another poster.

EXPECTATIONS OF LEADERS

Leads by example
Listens
Is fair
Is open to change
Encourages/Educates
Has patience
Helps develop skills (Empowerment)
Has a vision and communicates it

Keen could tell that people were evaluating themselves against the lists. "At the next meeting we'll elaborate and discuss any questions that you may have about any of the items on these lists."

Peter stood up and stretched. "We've made a lot of changes and covered a lot of ground during the past few years. We've also made a lot of progress, but we have a long way to go. Like most Westerners, we always want to look back and talk about how far we have come, instead of looking ahead to see how far there is to go. Does anyone have any questions or comments about anything?"

Fred Ulrich cleared his throat. "I want to share something with all of you that I read this morning which applies to our situation. It's about survival of the fittest. The article stated that the business world is similar to the natural world, in that survival of the fittest is the name of the game. When we study the evolutionary process of different species, we find that certain species have adapted to environmental changes better than others. In the business world, too, a company needs to adapt to changes in order to survive. This can mean learning new leadership skills, implementing JIT, TQM, or anything. Some people here at Magic, though, are still resisting the necessary changes. But we need to make these changes. We have to make them. Because if we don't, we're going to be out of business."

When Ulrich was finished, everyone looked to Peter for confirmation or reassurance. "Fred's right. But he's not just talking about us. He could be talking about any company anywhere in the world. American industry is in jeopardy from international competition. In order to compete internationally and at home, our productivity and waste elimination must increase. We have the potential to compete with any country in the world. But in order to compete and survive, we must have the commitment to manufacturing excellence. One affordable solution available to every American company lies in the various concepts that we're trying. Especially growing our associates through life long education.

"What does it take to become a world-class manufacturer? As we've learned, it's both simple and difficult. Simple, because the ways to improve our plant are many and the information is readily available. Difficult, because the path to world-class manufacturing requires all of us to accept and embrace change.

"Most of us resist change because it forces us to revise the comfortable behavior patterns we have built for ourselves in our daily lives. But the simple fact is that the world competitors down the road are learning to deal with change. They have learned how to be flexible in their operations, with their customers and suppliers as well as with their employees. Companies that learn and accept change as the only constraint in their environment truly have a competitive edge. More and more of America's industry is waking up to the fact that the best way to deal with change is to make it a part of our everyday existence—to expect it, to accept it, even to enjoy it.

"The path to world-class manufacturing excellence begins with knowledge and ideas. Your ideas. Your knowledge. Remember, knowledge is power."

Just then Gina, the receptionist, came into the room to give Chet a message. Everyone could tell that something was wrong. Five minutes after the meeting, Chet, Peter, and Fred were discussing a quality problem discovered by a major customer. The gestures and body language showed that they were making some serious and quick decisions.

"We'll have to send three people over to sort parts immediately," Fred said. "Next, we'll have to start running new parts so they won't run out."

Peter and Chet agreed, and things were set in motion. Another situation was handled in an efficient and expedient manner, a tribute to the improved communication and planning that had gone on in the months before.

14

Leadership Should Have the Capacity to Educate

"Lets All Think Like a Customer"

Things were moving fast at Magic. Keen could hardly believe how much ground they had covered in three years. So much information, so many new ideas—were they taking root? He was especially curious about the new definition of leadership he was building. Were the leads ready to stop being supervisors—as Peter had suggested—and start becoming leaders? Keen felt it was time to find out about that in particular. He would start there anyway. Somehow the meetings at Magic seemed to wander to the topics most important to everyone, no matter what the original plan was. "Hello, leads," the professor said to the group, imitating an elementary school teacher.

"Hello, professor," a few replied jokingly. Everyone was laughing.

"What a great way to start a meeting," Keen bellowed, looking up at the ceiling and holding his hands over his head. "Just look at us. We're laughing. We're smiling. We're excited to be here. Isn't life grand?" Still smiling, he looked at the group and asked, "Tell me, how do you cultivate leadership skills?"

"Say what?" someone asked. The laughter stopped, and all eyes were on the professor. Keen decided to rephrase his question. "Everyone in this room is a leader." He emphasized the word *leader* with a deep, exaggerated voice. "Each of you is a lead. A coach. And each one of you has demonstrated your leadership skills on the shop floor. So tell me, what have you learned over the past several weeks?"

"The one thing I've learned is that you have to earn the right to be followed," said Scott, from the spring department. "Also, you can't wait for others to solve your problems."

"Regarding problems, they don't just go away," said Peter. "Problems should be killed, not just wounded."

Scott and the others knew exactly what Peter meant.

"I believe you need to understand and clarify your own values so that you can put them into practice and set priorities to fill your goals," said Ashley. "You have to let your conviction show."

"Great. What else?"

Courtney raised her hand. Keen looked at her and smiled. She still frequently raised her hand to be called on instead of just speaking out. "In one of our first meetings, you explained how we must learn to tolerate conflict and disagreement," she said. "We also learned that we should use conflict as a source of information, rather than treating it as a threat."

"Have you practiced that skill on the shop floor?"

"Yes, I have," Courtney stated. "And I've noticed an incredible difference."

"I have, too," one of the other leads replied.

"Good, good," said Keen. "But there is something I want each of you to remember. We are all, to some degree, mismanagers. By that I mean that we cannot see every side of a situation when we act alone. That's why the leadership skills you're learning are so important. Another thing I want all of you to keep in mind is that we are all imperfect. No matter how many meetings we hold or how much training we receive, we will never be perfect. And neither will the people in your departments. We cannot expect perfection of ourselves or those around us."

Brian cleared his throat and added, "Professor, you're right. Nobody's perfect, we never will be perfect, and we can't expect perfection in others. But we need to be ready to recognize excellence in others and to accept it from both our peers and our subordinates. I've been seeing a whole lot of what I would classify as excellence in others. I've seen a lot of workers improving their setup time, housekeeping habits, and other things. I've also seen a lot of leads exhibiting excellence in their leadership skills, and I think we should recognize that."

Peter remarked, "What's so important here is the fact that everyone is noticing these improvements and that you're using these new leadership skills. And the people in your departments may not realize what the change is, but they're reacting to the changes. Even though they may not consciously see the difference, they feel it and they're responding to it. Your actions are causing positive reactions throughout the plant."

"I've learned something from these meetings that I feel is important," said Fred Ulrich. "An essential factor in leadership is the capacity to educate the members of the organization."

"Do you feel we have this capacity?" Asked Keen.

"I know we have it," Ulrich proudly exclaimed. "And as we continue to learn and to grow I think we'll see even more of it come out."

"I have something I'd like to share," said Peter. "If you take the time to communicate to the people in your department why a job is important and how it serves the customer, you often will improve their attitude and work quality."

"Peter, I agree with you," Scott said hesitantly. "Maybe it's just me, but I'm not sure I know exactly how some of these jobs serve the customer."

"I don't either," someone else chimed in.

"Neither do I," came another.

Peter looked at the group. "I think we've found another topic here that we need to learn more about. That's why these meetings are so important. We'll never learn all there is to know. It has to be a continuous process. Remember that a learning organization is fundamentally an organization that practices continuous improvement and continually enhances its capacity to create its own future. And that's what we are doing here. We're creating our own future."

No one understood exactly what Peter meant, but they all got the drift.

"Scott, you brought up a very good point," Peter continued. "Let's think about this. How does each job serve the customer? Many of us take for granted that we know the answer, when, in fact, we don't." Peter stopped, thought for a moment, then resumed. "Each of us needs to view the work we're doing in our department from the perspective of our internal and external customers. We need to think like the customer."

Keen allowed time for Peter's comments to sink in and make an impact on everyone. Then he asked, "*Do we have any imposed customers?*"

"We've never heard of that," Scott remarked.

"Ed Deming pointed out that this is the most demanding and devastating customer of all," explained the professor. "An imposed customer is someone, like a boss, who informally imposes counterproductive rules and actions on the group. Let me give you an example." Keen thought for a moment. "Anyone here ever ship a part that wasn't quite up to specs, but some boss said ship it anyway?"

"Yea, occasionally," responded several leads, as laughter broke out.

"What is the expectation of Magic regarding quality parts?" the professor asked.

"Only ship quality parts that meet all the customer's requirements on time," replied Ulrich.

"Then why do we occasionally ship parts that aren't meeting specifications?" queried the professor.

"Because the customer needs them and the boss says they'll use them since they need them bad enough," said Courtney, as she glanced over at Peter to see what his reaction was to these questions and answers.

"Oh, you mean that the customer has a moving range of quality when it comes to crunch time?" Keen asked.

"That's life in the real world, professor," someone retorted.

"Is this really quality?" Keen was going to flush out some answers. "Or is it that we don't know how to kill a bad process in our system? Aren't we really placing Band-Aids on the problems? We're doing things right by supposedly serving the external customer. But is it really the right thing?"

"You're point is valid," Ulrich replied. "But as someone said a moment ago, we're dealing with the real world."

Peter joined the discussion. "Do you remember seeing on the videos and reading that world-class manufacturers stop the production line and fix the problem before shipping any parts that don't meet quality measurements? They are doing the right thing. How many times will they be faced with that same problem in the future?"

"It seems to me that they may have killed the problem once and for all," said Ashley.

"How do you think the workers feel when they know that they never have to worry about that problem again?" Keen asked.

"It would be a good feeling," someone replied. "And that's the way it should be, but it isn't realistic. Is it?"

"Does this mean that we have imposed on ourselves a constraint to be less than world class?" asked Keen.

"All right, professor, you've made your point," admitted Fred Ulrich. "We need to have the courage to face reality as it is. I know, the first prerequisite for common sense."

Peter stood up and walked around the room. "Let's look at some basic business logic. I have a question for you. Do we make products?"

"Yes," a few leads replied.

"We think we are making products. But our customers think they are buying services. Do you see the difference? From the customer's standpoint, a product is nothing more than a tangible means for getting a service performed."

Peter did not expect everyone to comprehend precisely what he was trying to explain, but he wanted them to at least give these theories some thought.

"What about mistakes?" he asked. "Since implementing our quality program and the other concepts, we've dramatically improved the quality of our products. And we've cut down on waste. But do we worry about mistakes?"

"Yes," came the unanimous reply.

"You're right. We do worry about the mistakes. But we can't just worry about the visible mistakes. If we only worry about the visible mistakes, then we'll lose customers because of the invisible mistakes."

The expressions on the leads' faces revealed that this bit of logic needed to be clarified. "A visible mistake is obvious, you can see the defect," said Courtney. "But what are invisible mistakes?"

"Invisible mistakes can include many factors that aren't obvious, such as failing to take risks, and failing to innovate in order to create new value for customers," explained Peter. "For example, many manufacturers hold the opinion that their technologies create products. But customers think their desires create products. A lot of manufacturers think they are market-oriented when they ask for their customers' opinions of products that already exist. But we need to ask our customers what their problems are. As a supplier, we need to stay ahead of our customers with our processes and products."

"Why don't we invite our customers to visit us here at Magic, to tour the plant and give us suggestions about the products they buy from us," interjected an overexcited Ashley. "We'll meet them and they'll meet us."

"I love it," Peter said. "At the next meeting I want to concentrate on how and when to invite our customers to visit our plant. If we can get our current customers into our plant we'll let our best sales tools—our associates—convince them to do business with us."

"Why stop with current customers," asked Lee from the sales department. "Why not invite potential customers?"

"We can show them what we're doing," a machinist proudly stated.

"Yea, and we can show off our housekeeping and some of our new machines," someone else said.

"It'll be a great morale booster for the workers," Scott threw in.

"I see it as a win-win situation," Ulrich exclaimed. "Oh, I've got another idea. We should have a suppliers' day, too."

Peter gave everyone a challenge. "For the next several days, let's all think like a customer. We need to see things from their perspective. How do they view the plant, our products, and us? After all, without customers there would be no Magic Manufacturing."

15

Safety and Maintenance

"This Is Just the Tip of the Iceberg as to The Brain Power of the Workers"

Over the horizon another beautiful sun was rising. As Peter drove into the parking lot, he thought to himself that he needed to address the energy vampires. He and Keen had counseled the leads and spoken directly to them about the need to change. But the time had come to ask some to leave. It had become evident that Tom, pressroom foreman, would not fit the culture, and, worse yet, that he was not going to try. In the spirit of TRIC, Tom and Chet agreed that Tom could have sixty days to look for a job with several conditions: No one was to know he was looking; there was to be no badmouthing of Magic or its people; and Tom must keep Chet informed of his job search.

Peter noticed that Keen's car was there. Keen had been out of the country for several weeks and was chomping at the bit to get back into the swing of things at Magic. He had arrived back in town two days ago and had called Peter three times since his return. Peter looked forward to seeing his friend this morning, and they had agreed to meet to talk about the quality of life issues and to bring the professor up to date.

Peter enjoyed meeting with the professor because Keen was not afraid to ask any question. Sometimes the professor was like a pain in the backside, and sometimes he missed the target, but it was stimulating. This persistent questioning was a blessing in disguise because it did cause people to follow through. Likewise, Peter enjoyed disagreeing with Keen about the differences between the real world and the academic one. They complemented each other.

In reminiscing for a few moments, Peter recalled one of the first differences they had discussed. Keen had thought that Magic's main difficulty was not adhering to a fixed production schedule. Keen's solution was to hold sacred the first three or four days of each week as to the schedule, and use the other days as flexible scheduling time for unexpected customer demand. Keen just did not understand that Magic had to jump through hoops on very short notice to serve its customers' unexpected demands. This was one feature that Magic was already well known for. In fact, it was a niche that the company had developed and built its reputation on. Keen wanted to tell the customer, "you have to get in a queue until our flex schedule day arrives." Magic's customers would have said good-bye and looked for a more cooperative supplier.

Peter's reminiscing stopped when he turned the corner leading into the eating area, and he saw Keen talking to Fred and drinking some coffee.

"Good morning, professor," smiled Peter. "Any new theories for us today?"

"You never know," said Keen.

Fred laughed and said, "We've been talking about some of our dream killers. We should certainly get rid of them."

"You're right," Peter said. "We need to purge the bad apples. It isn't fair to the rest of the people here."

Fred nodded his head in agreement. "I have to get back on the floor to see how things are going. See you later."

On the way to Peter's office, Peter and Keen spent a few minutes catching up on the major news items and what was happening with their kids before they got to talking shop.

"I know the first question that you'll challenge me with this morning, and I'm ready for you," said Peter, with his classic grin. "Housekeeping, safety, preventive maintenance, and problem solving—the four areas pertaining to helping our people grow. How's that for hitting the target?"

"I'd say you hit the bull's-eye," Keen replied. "But you do know there are moving targets, don't you? Just like there are moving schedules. On a more serious note, though, I did notice that the housekeeping is getting better and better."

"I'm glad you noticed. Harry, our accountant, and the housekeeping focus groups have developed an audit sheet for each area of the company."

"Are you satisfied with the improvement?"

Peter pondered the question. "Let's say we have done a lot, but I still see lots of room for improvement."

"What's your gut feeling about the workers' attitude toward the housekeeping results?"

"I believe that they have taken pride in it. On several occasions, I've seen people reminding others to clean up after themselves. Before, no one said anything about organization or cleanliness. Even outside, I've seen people pick up trash that had blown into the parking lots and carry it to their car or bring it into the company to put in a trash container."

While walking through the plant, Keen had seen evidence of more pride in housekeeping. He, too, had observed several workers going above and beyond just picking up after themselves.

"Are you still cleaning the bathrooms?" Keen inquired.

"No. We've hired someone to do that. She's a fanatic about keeping the common areas clean. She also reminds others to pick up after themselves if they forget."

"Are you receiving any comments from visitors about the way the place looks?"

"All the time. And it's really helped our people want to keep it looking nice. In fact, I remember when we used to have an all-points-bulletin for cleanup, because we had someone visiting us that we wanted to impress. The workers knew what was going on and would clean up. Now the place is always clean and organized. Plus, hearing this from people outside our organization helps to reinforce what we are doing. They've really taken pride and ownership in housekeeping."

"Would it be fair to say that they have grown as people?"

"No doubt about it," Peter responded without any hesitation.

"How do you assess the progress of the safety focus group?"

"We haven't adopted your suggestion of a safety board, but we have done some neat things to raise everyone's awareness concerning safety." Peter teasingly asked, "Would you like to know what they are?"

Keen smiled.

"I did find out that many individuals weren't very safety conscious. So we made sure that everyone knows who is on the safety focus committee."

"How did you do this?"

"In our departmental meetings, we discussed who was on the committee. And we posted the pictures of all focus committee members on all the information boards. We've also encouraged everyone to discuss any safety idea with any or all members of the committe."

Keen asked, "Has the committee done anything else?"

"They investigated what a few other companies were doing and added a few ideas of their own to the process. My goal is to make everyone aware of safety daily. One of the first things the committee did was to buy large pins or buttons with Magic's logo on them as well as a statement that claims 'Safety Counts.' They then developed a game with it. During a two-week period they assigned someone to draw one name out of a hat that contained the names of all our employees. This person chooses any day within this two week time window to have a name drawn out of the hat. Then the person goes to check to see if the employee whose name was drawn is wearing his or her 'Safety Counts' button. If this person finds the employee wearing the safety button, that employee is awarded a $25 gift certificate to Wal-Mart. We were going to give restaurant certificates but some people didn't like that idea. So far, we've had three winners and everyone seems to be happy with the gift certificate."

"What happens if the person isn't wearing the button?"

"Then we keep drawing until we find someone wearing a button. Then we post the name of the winner plus the names of the people who were not wearing their buttons."

"Now I know why everyone is wearing those buttons," Keen remarked. "Can I have one, too?"

"Always trying to make money, aren't you?" grinned Peter.

"Can't blame a fellow for trying," Keen smiled back. "Is there anything else that they have done as of now?"

"As a matter of fact, there is. They have another game that's associated with bingo cards."

"Bingo cards? How does that work?"

"Everyone is assigned to a team. The teams are heterogeneous in that the office and other support functions, such as quality assurance and production, are all combined. This is because the office usually has fewer accidents and safety issues. It wouldn't be fair to just have the office as a team because the probability of having an accident is low.

"Each member of the team is given a bingo card with the different numbers on it. The objective is to complete the bingo card. All the different versions of bingo are used, such as a straight line, diagonal line, postage stamp on the corners or around the free space, complete the whole card, and any other version they can create. By varying the games it does create more interest."

Keen was intently listening to every word, but he was slightly confused. "How does this tie into safety?"

"Remember, each employee is a member of a team."

"I recall you saying that but . . ."

"You cannot use the daily number drawn for your card if anyone on your team has an accident that day," explained Peter, "Furthermore, if anyone on your team has an accident that requires outside medical attention, you cannot use any of the numbers drawn that week toward your bingo card."

"Isn't that kind of inviting the employees to cover up accidents?"

"You might think of it that way," Peter said. "But we hope and trust that all accidents are taken care of immediately. Over and over we remind everyone that their safety is most important and ask them to please get immediate attention if something happens. Also, I don't believe if someone is hurt that he or she won't seek help."

"What is the reward if you win the bingo game?"

"The dollar amounts vary depending on the game being played. For five in a row or a postage stamp the winner receives a $10 to $25 gift certificate to Wal-Mart. When we play cover the whole card, we award $50 to the first two who complete their cards. Since the dollar amount doesn't come close to winning the lotto, I feel that since the financial incentive is so modest workers won't risk their safety or jeopardize their health by not seeking help if an accident occurs."

"How's it been going to date?"

"We've had a lot of success with it. Everyone seems to be enjoying the games and it has made everybody more sensitive about safety. I'm very pleased as to the progress. By the way, did you know our bingo program had to be registered with the state? It is the law."

"No," Keen said. "Have you noticed any peer pressure to have the team members be more safe?"

"Questions, questions, questions," thought Peter. "Oh well, that's the professor's style. And he does bring up some imperative points to consider."

Peter then returned to the conversation. "I'm not sure how much of that actually goes on but I do know that everyone is looking at the master bingo card everyday in the eating room to see what number has been drawn that day. And I'm assuming that individually they are sensitive to letting the team down. Indirectly, I would have to say there is probably some peer pressure."

Keen slowly shook his head as he shrugged his shoulders. "I'm not sure. But, according to the results, it seems that everyone is more safety conscious and that accidents are down, which is impressive. My compliments to you."

"John, do me a favor."

"Sure."

"Tell the safety committee the same thing."

"Excellent suggestion. I'll do it soon."

"Thanks."

Peter was looking at a bingo card and suddenly remembered something else. "One more thing about the bingo game," he began. "The focus committee decided that if there was an accident and there was lost time at work, then the bingo game wouldn't be played for two weeks. They thought that all these different incentives would make everyone more sensitive to being safe."

"I'm impressed at what the safety committee has invented on its own." Keen was blown away by the strides made by the workers. "What can I say?"

The room was quiet for a moment. Then Keen asked, "By the way, how did you come by 'Big John?'"

"You mean that life-size poster of a worker next to the eating room?"

"Yes."

"I saw that while taking a tour of one of the companies that I network with through the local Chamber of Commerce. I found out where to buy one and asked the focus committee what they thought. Their overwhelming response was 'great.' So, we got one."

"How does it work?"

Whenever an accident occurs, we type out the date of the accident and the name of the person who was injured," Peter explained. "We then place this information on the picture of Big John's body where the worker actually got hurt. It's like a Pareto analysis. By looking at Big John's body, you see where most of the injuries have occurred. And just like in a Pareto analysis, we focus to eliminate the injuries, especially in the area where most of them have happened."

"Now I see why you placed Big John near the eating room," Keen responded. "Everyone walks by it quite often, which makes people more aware of being careful."

Peter smiled. "The location was also the committee's idea for that same reason. They wanted Big John's presence to be felt."

"Excuse me, do you have a minute?" Larry, the maintenance lead, asked.

"Of course we do," Peter replied. "What's up?"

"Well, we've been discussing the importance and benefits of having a strong preventive maintenance program. I know how the workers become frustrated when they have to call me and wait until someone can get to helping them. However, worse than that is when they complain about me not fixing something. The problem is they never tell us it has to be fixed. They just keep trying to make do the best they can until their machine completely stops working. We all know what that does to shipping pressures around here. Anyway, over the weekend I came up with an idea of how we might stay ahead of most of these problems."

Peter was delighted in what he was hearing. His maintenance lead spent his weekend thinking of ways to improve his job and the quality of life for everyone. Peter was thinking of how many good people work at Magic, who are willing to give of their personal time.

"Larry, that's terrific," Peter exclaimed. "Please share it with us."

Larry's face was flushed and he had a glow in his eyes as he broke into a broad grin. "I'd like to. Can you spare a few minutes and come back to my workbench? It'll be easier to show you how it works rather than trying to explain it without seeing what I'm proposing."

Peter and Keen followed Larry to his workbench area which was about 10 feet by 15 feet. It was immaculate. Every tool was in its place. The floor was spotless. And mounted on the wall was a large red board. Larry stood in front of the board.

"I've come up with a concept that I propose to call 'Red Tag It,'" Larry said, pointing to the board.

"The Red Tag It," Keen and Peter almost said in unison." How does it work?"

Larry cleared his throat because of being a little nervous at this time. "Well, when anyone finds something that isn't working properly the person should hang or somehow put a red tag on it. Then I am proposing that the person fill out this multi-copy form with a date, what the problem is, and, if possible draw a simple picture of what isn't right. Then the form should be placedin Chet's in-box."

"Chet's?" questioned Keen.

"Yes," Larry continued. "Since Chet is the plant manager and has the responsibility for scheduling all the work done on the floor, he needs to schedule time to fix each problem within 30 days of the date on the form."

"Why Chet?" Keen asked.

"I think I can answer that," said Peter. "Because Chet needs to schedule when he can best allow you to work on certain machines."

"That's right," Larry said. "Chet needs to provide us some hours to get to the problem. Currently, it sometimes takes weeks or months for things to get fixed. And, other times things get a quick fix, just to have them break down again the next week."

"That makes a lot of sense," said Keen.

Peter added, "It also makes more sense because Chet has a list that shows all the jobs he has to get through the plant each week and for the month. If one of these 'Red Tag It' items gets on that form, we'll all see it at our weekly review meetings. This will be a good reminder of what has to be done. I like it, Larry. I like it a lot."

Larry was feeling good about himself. He went on and explained, "Another thing that happens is these 'five minute fixes' the workers do themselves."

"What do you mean by 'five minute fixes'?" asked Keen.

"That's when a worker takes a few minutes every day and continually fixes the same thing over and over. What I'd like to do is fix this problem so the worker doesn't waste five or so minutes each day fixing the same thing over and over. I figured that if a worker spends five minutes a day tightening a fastener on a machine, in one year's time that adds up to be 1,250 minutes or 20 hours of work time. Isn't that the nonvalue added kind of stuff you've been talking about?"

Peter couldn't contain himself, "Larry, if we had more like you we could conquer the world!"

Larry, a bashful sort, turned red and looked scared. "I'll pass on that," he stammered.

Keen and Peter burst into laughter.

"Larry, it's only a figure of speech," Peter teased. "However, I can't compliment you enough for what you've come up with for our company and the workers. Thank you."

"You're welcome," replied Larry.

Keen spoke up and said, "Larry, I am impressed and compliment you, too. Why did you choose 30 days? Why not 15 days?"

"John, we have to start somewhere," Larry explained. "I think this will be challenging enough. However, I agree with you in that some time down the road we should consider lowering the time period. That's Kaizen, isn't it?"

"Larry, you are a special one," Keen said.

The smile on Larry's face said it all. He was in the clouds.

"What do we need to get it going?" asked Peter.

"Not really anything, except to have Chet and everyone buy into it," said Larry.

"I'll talk to Chet about this, but I want you to share with him what you just told us," Peter said. "We'll have you discuss this at our lead meeting. Then the leads can educate everyone else in their departmental meetings."

Peter thrust out his hand to shake Larry's hand and to congratulate him. "These are the kinds of ideas that are moving us along on our world-class journey," Peter told Larry.

The expression on Larry's face was worth a thousand words.

Keen and Peter thanked Larry and took their cold coffee back to Peter's office. They would gladly enjoy cold coffee any day for this type of action.

Peter was the first to speak. "What do you think?"

"Unbelievable," responded Keen.

Keen started rubbing the same part of his head again and Peter knew what was about to happen. "Didn't we discuss earlier that someone somehow would invent how to move on our preventive maintenance focus? *This is just the tip of the iceberg as to the brain power of the workers.* It will only get better as time goes on and the culture of growing people takes deeper roots."

"I can hardly wait to find out what happens next."

"Have you had a chance to check with some of the other companies to find out what they are doing about problem solving?" asked Keen.

"Yes, I have. I've spoken to several of them, and none seem to have any standard one best way of how to go about doing this. Some use their suggestion boxes as one way, while others brainstorm with managers and workers as to what might be done to improve things. But I haven't found anything that excites me, yet. What about you?"

"Same here. I found a couple of brainstorming techniques, but I think we should continue to investigate more."

Peter agreed that they needed to make more inquiries. Then Peter asked if there was any more to discuss on the quality of life issues.

"What do you think of celebrations?" Keen asked.

97

"I like them."

"What I mean is celebrations at work."

"I know what you mean," said Peter.

"Do you have any ideas along this line?"

Peter shook his head to indicate that he did not.

"What do you think of establishing some type of a focus group to see what kind of things we might consider doing at Magic?" asked Keen.

"Let me think about it," stated Peter. "I am a little concerned about all of these meetings and hours away from production. I won't rule it out, though."

"To me, celebrations are a way of recognizing the thousands of good things that go on every day at work. It helps build pride in the accomplishments of what you are all doing collectively and, consequently, for the company."

"I don't disagree with you," Peter declared. "But let me think about it."

"Fair enough."

"It seems like we've covered the waterfront regarding the quality of life issues this morning. Anything else?" asked Peter.

"Not really on this subject. But I would like to get your reaction as to what is happening at the university."

The phone rang and Peter picked it up. "Thank you," he said into the telephone. "I forgot that they were coming today. Tell them I'll be there in a couple of minutes."

He then hung up the receiver. "John, I'm sorry but this Japanese company that we've been trying to establish a working relationship with has three people in the lobby waiting for me. I thought we had enough time. Larry's input today consumed some of our time. I know this issue of teaching these ideas is important to you. It's also important to me. We'll do it soon if that's okay with you."

"I understand. This is something like a flex schedule. Isn't it?"

"You're learning," responded Peter.

"Have a good day. See you soon."

The following week, when Keen came to conduct a meeting at the plant, he couldn't believe his eyes. The machines looked like they were decorated for Christmas. There were red tags everywhere. He walked back to Larry's board and it was filled to capacity.

Larry came up to Keen, smiling. "Hello, professor. Did you notice the red tags on the machines?"

"How could I not see them. They're everywhere."

Larry's smile reached from ear to ear. "I guess you could say the 'Red Tag It' system caught on quite fast."

The professor shook Larry's hand, and nothing more needed to be said.

16

Discipline

There was spring fever inside the plant. The freshness of the new season seemed to have spilled over into almost every Magic employee. People were feeling good about themselves. Keen could not wait for his next meeting at Magic. Seeds were to be planted. Keen was going to the heart of growing people and their self-worth.

He was pleased with how receptive and enthusiastic the leads had been. Everyone looked forward to these learning sessions with an open mind, and a mutual respect permeated the meetings. Each meeting was a learning experience for Keen as well as the leads. The practical questions asked and shared during these meetings were not only uniting the leads but also educating the professor. Keen knew that no textbook, magazine article, or conference could ever teach him as much as he was learning at Magic. Synthesizing and organizing the world-class ideas presented in books into a practical, workable format had been a blessing in so many ways. He was really grateful to Peter for believing in him and giving him a chance to work with Magic. Keen smiled to himself, and he was still smiling when he stood up to address the leads in the room that had been remodeled into a world-class learning center. No more wobbly chairs and torn plastic shower curtains.

"*Is discipline good or bad?*" he asked.

Some leads shouted back "good," and others "bad."

Keen grinned and said, "I seem to hear our usual consensus answer on this question."

The leads smiled, because they knew that somehow and some way the ol' professor was on his game and would pull an answer from them.

The professor shouted, "*Anyone who doesn't provide discipline is a cheat, thief, robber, and a person with less than full integrity.*" As he said this he flung his hands in various directions.

101

Everyone was on alert now, trying to sort out what had just been said. Bert, a machinist and second lead, spoke up. "Aren't you a little bit too strong about this?"

Keen smiled. "Do you feel I didn't say it loud enough?"

"You were loud and clear," said Bert. "But I don't see how you can say what you just did."

Sandy from the wire department explained, "If you're going to turn bad apples into better apples, you have to straighten them out first. They have to be disciplined. Because if you don't discipline them, you're robbing the rest of us of the type of company and work environment we all want."

"That's an interesting observation," retorted Keen. He then asked, "Being a disciple means what?"

Phil replied, "A disciple is a person trying to spread beliefs that he or she feels is right to other people."

"Very good," declared Keen. "Does anyone have any idea if and how *disciple* and *discipline* are related?"

There was no reply. Keen continued. "I have been curious about this and finally looked it up in the dictionary. The first thing I discovered was that the word discipline follows disciple in the dictionary. Also, a definition for disciple is 'one who receives instruction from another.' An additional part of the definition that I read was 'one who teaches or trains others.' Furthermore, the dictionary indicates that the obsolete meaning of disciple was 'punish or discipline.' Does this give anyone an idea why I can say that if you don't provide discipline you are thief and a cheat, and a person lacking full integrity?" asked the professor.

There was a long silence again. Keen went back to his seat. "How many here grew up believing that discipline was bad?"

Almost everyone raised a hand.

"So did I," responded Keen. "Do you recall some statements like these from your childhood? 'Just wait till your father gets home, he'll discipline you for saying that. Wait till your Mom finds out, she'll discipline you for this.' Or do you remember your third-grade teacher saying that when she tells your parents about your behavior you'll be disciplined?"

Larry laughed and said, "How come you know so much about our past?"

"We've all experienced this in one form or another," Keen explained. "Our parents, teachers, ministers, and friends were saying what they thought to be correct."

"So discipline is more than punishment?" Ashley questioningly repeated, so as to reconfirm what she had just heard.

"It sure is," confirmed Keen. "Ashley, do you like to discipline workers?"

"Not really," Ashley responded. "That is, unless they've done something serious that could harm someone or damage some equipment or machine. It is one thing I really hate about being a supervisor or lead. It is my least favorite thing to do."

"Okay," said Keen. "What about you Scott?"

"No. I don't like to discipline people either."

"Does anyone here like to take disciplinary action against workers?" Keen asked. The room was silent. "That's what I thought. For many leads, discipline is the worst part of their job. They hate to have to discipline others. We're not comfortable doing it." The professor looked around the room. "How come?"

Ashley asked, "Is it because we have never learned how to do it?"

"That's certainly a big part of it," said Keen. "How can I hone my skills and become a better person or worker if I am not instructed how to do things properly?"

"You can't," said Larry.

"That's correct! I can't get better if someone doesn't coach, mentor, teach, or help me change my behavior or habits. That's why I say you're a robber and a cheat and lack full integrity. I want to grow as an individual and increase my self-esteem, and you are robbing me of an opportunity to do so if you don't discipline me."

Keen was learning as he was teaching. "Discipline is not so much punishment as it is helping people grow. We need to teach everyone at Magic that this is the real meaning and value of discipline."

"I do believe in counseling before consequences. We have to provide people plenty of opportunities to change," Peter agreed. "Only after trying to teach someone new habits and ways of doing things and finding that the person still won't change should the individual be invited to work elsewhere."

"Let's take a few moments to look at discipline as we probably learned it and possibly practice it today," Keen suggested. "What do many people do to keep people in line?"

"You've got to establish penalties for inadequate performance," replied Chris.

"True," Keen said. "But only after counseling."

The professor paused. Then continued. "Penalties may prevent what you don't want, but you won't get much more than that," he explained. "This is sometimes known as the 'punishment effect.' Companies that don't train and educate their people about the idea of discipline as a growth concept many times experience that effect."

"Dr. Keen, what exactly is this 'punishment effect' thing?" Chris asked.

"When punishment is used to control people's behavior, most of the time people perform at a level just sufficient to avoid punishment," Keen answered. "Let me give you an example. I assume that everyone here drives. You are all well aware of speed limits. How fast do you usually drive in a fifty-five mile-per-hour zone?"

There was some laughter and several different comments. Many replied between sixty and sixth-five miles-per-hour.

"How come you exceed the speed limit?" asked Keen.

Sandy responded for the group when she said, "If you drive faster than sixty-five, you get an expensive ticket and your insurance goes up."

"I think many drive at a speed just short of the point where they think they might get caught or punished—the punishment effect," Keen stated. He could see from people's expressions that they understood.

"*Punishment should be our last action in trying to change behavior.* In reality, the person should be on the edge of being dismissed at this time."

"So discipline can be positive?" someone asked.

"Right on!" Keen was gratified. "That's certainly the attitude we want to develop at Magic." The professor had made his point and everyone was starting to internalize it.

"Another problem with discipline comes when we're talking about participative management and empowerment," said Peter from the back of the room. "If I empower you as team, does that mean that you can order pizzas for lunch and take longer lunch breaks?" he asked. "It's got to be within the framework and boundaries we have established for the company. When we empower you and the workers, it has to be within set boundaries. We need to continuously teach and remind people of their responsibilities."

"Peter just mentioned responsibility," said Keen. "We have to realize that response is the root of responsibility. It is our response to what is expected of us. Everyone wants to know what is expected. Who has the responsibility to let the workers know what is expected of them?"

"We do!" the leads responded.

"Another way to think of discipline is that we all have warts," said Keen, as he smiled at Peter. "We've all got some things in our lives that hurt us. We have sore spots. Right?"

A few of the leads were nodding their heads in agreement.

"What do we do about them?" Keen asked.

"We try to make them feel better by taking care of them?" someone responded.

"That's right," Keen smiled. "We should employ the same concept to helping people grow."

Peter was wondering how the professor was going to tie this together.

"*Do you have a chance of solving a problem if you never confront it?*" asked Keen. "Have you ever tried to provide the secret type of discipline by giving some worker the silent treatment for a few days?"

Laughter broke out.

"How about your spouse?" Keen asked. "How about your children? How about your neighbor? You just don't speak to them and give them some body language that is supposed to tell them that you are unhappy. How do you know if they even have a clue as to what you're upset about? How do you know their side of the story? Maybe your perception of the problem is not entirely correct. Is this adult or childlike behavior? How can one hope to grow in this type of culture? Discipline is training, providing instructions, changing behavior, changing habits, learning. How can I do this if you don't coach others to improve?

"As leads, you have to start to internalize the tremendous opportunity you have to help each other and everyone else grow by providing discipline," Keen pointed out. "You have to start to think in terms of discipline as a growth tool. As I hope you now understand, discipline is not a bogeyman."

"Professor, this all sounds good," said Barb, a second lead from the spring department. "But if I go out to the floor now and start this stuff, it will be a disaster."

"Why's that, Barb?" inquired Keen. He knew exactly where she was going, but he wanted her to say it for the group. He knew they were all thinking the same thing—how hard this would be to do and that they really did not look forward to doing it.

"I just don't feel like I can go out to my workers and start this discipline stuff. They won't understand where I'm coming from and they'll give me a rough time about it. So, what can I do?"

"Do you believe that discipline is important to growing one's self-esteem?"

"I do now, after listening to your explanation of it."

"Good. Would you feel better if all the workers heard a condensed version of what you have just heard this afternoon?"

"It certainly would help," responded several of the leads.

"Then we'll plan to do this soon, during one of our education sessions. I also would like to use our next few leads education meetings to share with you how to give and receive criticism. This will provide you with some tools to better handle discipline."

The time had flown by and the leads were leaving the new learning center when Peter asked Keen if he could talk to him for a few minutes before he headed home for dinner. "I am interested in what you mentioned about criticism. How many sessions do you feel you need for that?"

"I estimate about four. The first one will be an overview of criticism. Second, we'll give ideas and suggestions on how to give criticism. Third, we'll practice how to receive it. Finally, I'll discuss some traps and hints on how to take the sting out of criticism."

"This is really getting at the core of how to grow self-esteem, isn't it? I can see how every one of us can use this at home and everywhere we go."

"Peter, everything I try and bring to the Magic family is with the intention of making it compatible with everyone's personal, professional, social, and spiritual life."

"I know that," said Peter. "And what's more, all those dimensions of our lives at Magic are continually improving."

17

Lifelong Education

It's as if the Journey Never Ends, Or There Is
No Finish Line

Peter and Keen were sitting alone on a picnic table outside the plant. They were eating lunch and admiring the cleanliness of the parking lot and the grounds. Peter's emphasis on housekeeping had carried over into all areas of the company. "We've come a long way in the past few years, my friend," Peter said.

"Yes, we have. But we've just begun."

"I know. Still, there's been such a dramatic change in the atmosphere here. Especially in the way the leads have accepted the new concepts. I never thought I'd see such noticeable results so soon."

"The reason it's most noticeable in the leads is because they've been receiving the bulk of the education. Now we have to start educating the workers with the same intensity. Rightly so, we began by educating the management and the leads, and the workers to a lesser extent. At that time, that was the focus we needed to have. The Herbie sessions certainly helped to clear away many of the false perceptions that the workers had. Also, it provided them with an opportunity to raise additional concerns and to hear directly from you what your plans and focus areas were. You did an excellent job in laying the foundation for their wanting to know more, as well as in clearly articulating the 4+1 expectations. Now, the time has arrived to concentrate our efforts on educating all the associates as well as continuing to teach the managers and leads how to manage and lead."

"I agree," said Peter. "*It's as if the journey never ends, or there is no finish line.*"

"I've been giving it some thought. Maybe a good way to start would be to review our 4+1 focus and introduce the simple financial measurements discussed in *The Goal.*"

"I like that. I have given a lot of thought to this need for education. What do you think of calling it "lifelong education"?

"Peter, I think that's a great idea. That ties in perfectly with the personal, professional, social and spiritual realms of everyone's life. Whatever you decide to teach them will help them grow in one aspect, if not many, of their lives."

Peter said, with a big grin, "Why do you think I named it that?"

"Okay, you set me up for that one. Nice going, I like the idea."

"Thanks, John. I'll plan to announce it at our next plantwide meeting. By the way, we are going to start having these lifelong education sessions on the average of about one every other week."

"Who will be required to attend these sessions?"

"Everyone will be expected to be there. I plan to communicate to everyone the importance of educating our people—or should I say *growing* our people?"

"Who will teach these sessions?"

"I have an open mind on that. All of our managers will be given an opportunity to teach, our leads will also be given an opportunity to share their ways of approaching things. We'll use outside guest speakers when applicable on specific topics."

Peter went on to say that the classes would be approximately eighty percent work-related, experience and the other twenty percent would relate to their personal life—topics like gainsharing, health care, customer service, quit smoking programs, quality issues, physicals, technical issues, strategic plans, financial planning, flow charting, health and wellness, and problem solving. "There isn't much that I won't consider," Peter remarked.

"That's fascinating," Keen said. "Many owners would consider only education that is directly tied back to improving work skills and knowledge. "

"John, this will be nothing like how it was when I started trying to educate the employees five years ago when I bought Magic. I remember standing up and looking at a group of sixteen workers gathered in the old meeting room. I thanked each one of them for staying after work to listen to what I wanted to share. I told them that most of them would probably rather be punching out now and going home, but that this was very important to me.

"Someone asked if they were getting paid for this overtime," Peter said. "I wasn't sure who had asked the question, but it wasn't presented in an offensive manner. After all, it was a legitimate concern. My only thoughts were on the possibilities that this meeting held for Magic and for each person in attendance."

"What did you say?"

"I said yes. Each person would be paid for the time spent in the meetings. I explained that these meetings were important for the future of Magic—their future, my future, and the company's future. That we could make it—that we must make it—a better future. I told them that it was entirely up to us what we wanted the future to be. Each and every one of us."

Keen was impressed. "What did you do next?"

"It seemed like it took a long time, but I looked into the face of each person seated around the table. Men, women, young and old. Some married, some divorced, some single, some widowed. Many of their expressions displayed apprehension or fear or confusion about why they were there. They didn't know what to expect. This was a new experience for them."

Peter paused and looked up at the sky. A cloud had drifted in front of the sun and gave a momentary reprieve from the heat.

He then continued. "I told them that whether or not any of them realized it, they'd been a part of a process of change over the last few years. Think of the cleanliness of the shop floor and the bathrooms."

"What response did you get?"

"Some said yes. Some smiled. But most just stared straight ahead."

"Then what did you do?"

"I was not feeling good at this point, but I pushed on anyway. I reminded them that regardless of who thought what at this time, none of these changes would have been possible without meetings and training and education. I told them that now it was their turn. That we wanted to get them involved in everything going on here at Magic, which would include weekly department meetings with their supervisors. Additionally, I told them that from time to time we would have some special speakers in to speak to us on specific topics of interest to Magic."

"What kind of a reaction did you get to that?"

"As I recall, someone raised a hand to speak. I told them that they should feel free to speak and that they didn't have to raise their hands. Just to speak out."

Peter thought for a moment. "They wanted to know if they were going to have to take tests. I told them for the most part no. However, for some areas, testing might help everyone better understand what they needed to know. I then introduced the idea of wanting them to learn about SPC. To my pleasant surprise, when I asked the group how many would like to learn more about SPC, practically everyone in the room expressed an interest."

"Aren't you still having difficulties getting everyone who is trained in SPC to use it?"

"Yes," Peter said. "Hindsight has taught me that we didn't approach the workers' concerns first. Or that we weren't very good in following through on our expectation that they use SPC. But we are learning every day how to better approach things and grow people." And, he wanted to add, every day it is getting easier.

18

Culture

"By the Inch It's a Cinch, and By the Yard It's Hard"

Peter belonged to several different local and regional business organizations. He looked forward to these get-togethers because of the networking and the camaraderie. Many of the other members simply used the meetings as a social respite from the office, but not Peter. He usually tried to learn at least one new concept or idea at each of the monthly meeting.

As he was sitting with several other business owners at that day's CIUG meeting, someone congratulated Peter on the turnaround taking place at Magic. Several brief articles about different aspects of Magic had appeared in various trade publications and local newspapers. The employees and leads were receiving quite a bit of attention due to their efforts and the results they were achieving, and all of the attention was well deserved. Much of the media attention that Magic was receiving was the result of speeches given by Peter and new contracts being awarded to the company. Yet there still was work to do.

When Peter arrived at Magic after the luncheon meeting, he was still deep in thought. He was always looking ahead, restlessly dissatisfied with the present. How could he make sure that lifelong education became a permanent part of the company? Surely there was more to true education than attending classes. It went more deeply than that. Lifelong education grew out of lifelong curiosity, a deeply seated attitude about learning new things. He saw Chet walking across the parking lot, approached him, and fired a question at him.

"What do you think of the overall attitude of everyone here?"

"The attitude here? I think it's fine."

"Do you think we have an attitude problem?" Peter asked.

"No. Definitely not. Compared to other companies I have seen or heard about, this is heaven."

"Do the workers in general have bad attitudes?"

"No. Why do you ask?"

"Maybe attitude is the wrong word." Peter became lost in thought, and began scratching his head as if to get the brain cells working.

"What do you think of using the word *climate*," asked Chet, "or *culture*?"

"Culture? Culture encompasses everything that goes on here. From providing working conditions that are clean, safe, and neat, to being dedicated to making those 1,001 improvements that make the difference. Culture promotes continuous improvement and removes the fear of implementing new ideas. Culture encourages workers to take pride and ownership. So we're on the right track, but we probably need to spend more time reinforcing and enhancing culture, and in particular, making education part of our culture."

"Now I see what you mean. Do you think we can?"

"Oh, yes," said Peter. "I think we're already on our way in that direction, but we just need to make some more changes specifically affecting the culture mind-set. I believe everyone here has the ability and the willingness to change. And I can see that we're on the right track in creating a system to support the change.

"It's our responsibility to develop a nourishing environment that nurtures change. We've been doing this through training and education. Everyone is provided with the knowledge, skills, and resources to insure that change can occur."

"What if they don't want to learn?" asked Chet.

"We need to make it in their best interest to improve, but as the old expression goes, *you can lead a horse to water, but you can't make it drink.* Some will probably not change or adapt to our environment. We may have to ask them to leave."

"Oh!" Chet exclaimed. "That's what Professor Keen meant when he said that in order to change the culture or anything, one must be teachable."

"Yes. Everyone must also develop or have enough skills and self-esteem to make the necessary changes."

"What about willingness?" asked Chet.

"As for willingness, everyone must also be willing to change and to apply his or her abilities to cause the change to occur."

"What about changing the structure of how we do things?"

"That's what we've been doing. Changing our focus from techniques to people, and from supervision to leads or coaching. Look at how positively our shop floor talent reacts today to visitors and requests for changes. I wish I had started earlier taking videos of what this place was like a few years ago versus now. What you and I have been doing without fully appreciating it is changing the culture and people structure of Magic Manufacturing."

"That's the same thing that John Keen says in a different way," Chet commented. "*By the inch it's a cinch, and by the yard it's hard.* I see what we've been doing without even fully realizing it."

Both men paused for a moment, then Chet broke the silence. "How do you see all those quality of life issues fitting into helping us change the culture?"

"Dr. Deming, Dr. Juran, and others have referred to addressing first the quality of life or the work environment for the workers. It is my belief that the issues that we have been working on are a vital part of any procedural system we might have in place at any one time. Having these so-called soft or quality of life issues in place makes it likely, if not guarantees, that our technical and procedural changes will occur with as little resistance as possible. Look at all the feedback we get now when we implement things. Some of the things we've done in the last three years would never have gotten off the ground if we hadn't dealt with the quality of life issues straight away. What is your opinion about establishing a culture focus group to organize celebrations and events?"

"I like it," Chet said without hesitation.

"I do too, but I'm not sure if I want to tie our people up with any more meetings."

"It would take up some time, but I know that the workers and the leads enjoy the events we have now," said Chet. "They talk about them a lot both before and after they take place. Personally, I think it's a good morale booster. Of course, some people appreciate them more than others. But it seems that the more events, the better the morale."

Peter's mind drifted to his mother's enthusiasm for family-like events at Magic. She had known somehow that food and togetherness promoted other qualities, a kind of unity of purpose. Before she died, she had brought Polish food—kielbasa with rye bread and horseradish, golabki, kapusta, sauerkraut—to various events at the company.

"I hadn't even thought of it until you brought it up. I would like to try it. Couldn't we also tie this celebration motif of recognition, fun, and social events into our lifelong education programs that are helping people grow?"

"Chet! Terrific insight. Celebrations and education *do* go hand in hand if you think about it. Both of these ideas will foster and nurture growing an individual's self-worth."

Peter's mind was racing a thousand miles per hour. "What do you think of giving the culture focus group a budget to use for their group?"

"I'm sure that they'll find a way to spend it," Chet chuckled.

19

Financial Measurements

"Throughput, Operating Expenses and Inventory"

K een wanted to put on a superlative performance at his first lifelong education session. He was convinced more than ever that Peter's lifelong education program was the right thing to do. In the long run, it would not only make Magic more profitable, but more importantly it would put the question of survival out of everyone's mind. The fear of not surviving would become a distant part of Magic's tribal history.

Keen was prepared with plenty of his now-famous plastic overhead transparencies. Everyone knew that somehow he would pull from him or her the meaning of each transparency. The workers enjoyed this, because it made them a part of the process, and they liked to hear what other people had to say. Keen had the ability to pull together everyone's diverse opinions into some kind of a sensible summary.

Everything was arranged in the learning center as Keen awaited the arrival of the first group of people. The managers, leads, and workers were comingled into groups to accommodate production schedules, as well as to demonstrate that everybody was learning these concepts at the same time. This had a tendency to lessen the notion of "us and them." It also created an instant communication vernacular regarding the concepts, acronyms, and expressions.

"Good morning, professor," was the general greeting given Keen as people entered the room.

At the appointed time, Keen started the meeting. He was practicing what he taught: *we do not reward people for being late by waiting for them.* By now, very few people at Magic were late without a good reason.

Another reason for punctuality had been developed and bought into by the workers. Courtney had suggested a while ago that anyone late for a meeting put a quarter in piggy banks sitting on the conference tables. At the end of the year, the coins were given to a worthy cause. The associates chose an organization that distributed Christmas gifts to needy children. Somehow, the practice of someone shaking the bank for anyone late to deposit his or her contribution had quickly taken hold at Magic. This was another sign that Magic had become more than just a place to work.

"It's good to be with you this morning," declared Keen. "I am honored to be able to initiate the lifelong education sessions. Can someone help me figure out what I am supposed to do this morning?"

After a few moments, Chris said, "We're here to learn about all kinds of things."

"We need to understand more about what all this world-class stuff means," responded Charlie.

Scott remembered a statement made during a recent meeting. "Peter told us during our plant meeting that it had something to do with growing people."

"Thanks, Scott, for that insight. More ideas?"

After a few moments of silence Keen continued, "I hope that we will always verbalize with each other. *Verbalize means saying what's on your mind.* We have to listen to each other to learn from each other.

"My focus this morning is to review our 4+1 program and to introduce simple financial measurements to you. Would someone please start the ball rolling by sharing what 4+1 means?"

"Are those the things that Peter told us about in our Herbie feedback meetings?" asked Phil.

"I don't know because I wasn't there. Besides that, I would have forgotten by now because I am absentminded." Keen started to rub his head. Several people in the room smiled; they knew his tricks.

"Preventive maintenance," said Peggy.

Keen wrote it down on a clear plastic overhead transparency that was being projected onto the new screen in the learning center.

Before he finished writing, someone else said "housekeeping." Keen wrote it down.

"Sample board," said Courtney.

"Good," said Keen.

"Come on, someone. Can anyone help us with the last two?"

After a few seconds, Walter spoke up and said, "Material problems."

Keen smiled and wrote down the fourth item. He then raised one of his fingers and asked what the +1 stood for. There was a little longer pause before someone finally said "setup time reduction."

After several minutes of comments and questions back and forth, the group had provided the reasons for each of the five areas of focus and identified what was being done to improve each one of them. So Keen raised four fingers on one hand and one finger on the other hand and said, "When you see me do this what are you going to say?"

The answers came back in rapid order. "Setup time reduction, material problems, sample board, housekeeping and preventive maintenance."

The professor then placed a clean transparency on the projector and wrote:

NET PROFIT = $1,000,000

"Is this good or bad?" he asked.

A couple of people said good, but Ashley's comment was, "It depends."

"What do you mean by it depends?" Keen asked.

Ashley explained, "It would depend on how much you have to invest to earn the $1,000,000."

"If I have to invest $10 million or $1 billion, it makes a big difference," said Keen. "This is known as the rate of return on your investment. Let's use ROI to indicate this and NP for net profit."

Keen removed the cap from his green overhead transparency pen and wrote:

ROI = .10 OR .001

"All a company needs to know in order to determine whether it is doing well or poorly is to look at these two numbers," revealed Keen. "I'm a typical male and don't like to shop. I just want to go into a store, pick it out, pay for it, and get going. I have really not developed very good buying skills. I need your help. Will you help me?"

Most of the people in the room were confused. Finally, someone offered to help him.

"Thank you. I need it. You are going to accompany me to a humongous warehouse where they sell Money Making Machines."

Before he could continue, someone said, "I like it already." Laughter and a lot of wisecracks rolled out.

"I don't know what questions to ask the salesperson," Keen said. "Will you help me with the questions?"

"Sure," was the response.

The professor drew a boxlike picture on the plastic transparency. "Now, what questions should I ask in buying this Money Making Machine?"

"How much does it cost?" someone asked.

Keen wrote down "$10,000,000."

"What is its warranty?"

"For your lifetime," Keen wrote.

"How much money does it make?"

Keen wrote "$1,000" on the transparency.

"How long does it take to make the $1,000?"

Keen looked around the room. "Oh, you have to clarify the inquiry. Very good."

He then wrote down, "$1,000 per hour." "That's, let's see, about $2,000,000 per year."

"What other questions should I ask?"

"How much does it cost to keep the machine going?" Sandy brought up.

Keen wrote "$2,000" on the transparency.

"What does the $2,000 mean?" asked Scott.

"Didn't I answer the question?" inquired the professor.

"Yes," said Scott. "But it isn't complete."

"Oh," Keen said coyly. "You mean the question to me was incomplete?"

"I guess it was," admitted Scott.

"Then what should the question have been?" asked Keen.

"How much does it cost to operate the machine each hour, day, week, or whatever?" responded Sandy.

"Excellent," exclaimed Keen. "What I have tried to teach you is that we have to be careful in how we ask questions or we will get incomplete information. This can also lead to misunderstandings and work being done the wrong way."

Keen continued. "The reason I needed your help in buying a Money Making Machine was to establish financial measurements that we can all use everyday. That is, **THROUGHPUT (T)** which was about $2,000,000, or the cash coming in, or the 'chi-ching' sound; **OPERATING EXPENSES**

(OE), which are the dollars that turn the wheels of the company (and we said that was $2,000 but didn't say it was for a day); and finally, the INVESTMENT (I) of $10,000,000, dollars stuck in the belly of the company. Those are the only financial measurements we ever have to know in order to help Magic make money.

"Now, we can complete our financial system," he said as he wrote:

$$NP = T - OE$$
$$ROI = \frac{T - OE}{I}$$

The professor saw that the class was following him, even though very few knew anything about accounting. "We can also determine how well Magic is doing regarding its two principal financial statements," explained Keen. "Banks like to see these two statements for loan purposes, and the IRS likes to see them for taxes."

Keen removed the transparency and placed another one on the overhead.

THE PRODUCTIVITY OF CAPITAL (Balance Sheet) can be measured by:
$$\frac{T}{I}$$

THE PRODUCTIVITY OF OPERATIONS (Income Statement) can be measured by:
$$\frac{T}{OE}$$

Furthermore, CASH FLOW can be determined by:
$$T - OE(+ \text{ or } -) \Delta \text{ in I}$$

Scott asked what the triangle meant.

"That is known as a Greek Delta for change," explained Keen. "So it means plus or minus the change in the investment." He then went on to explain that T, I, and OE could be considered as measurements that could be used by everyone.

"Let me give you a test," the professor said. He could tell from the expressions of several people in the group that they did not like taking tests. "Which direction do you want T to go? Up or down?"

"Up," was the loud response.

"Which direction do you want I and OE to go?"

"Down," a loud chorus exclaimed.

"You've now mastered the financial system of Magic," Keen said. "Every day, ask yourself this question: What can I do to get T to increase and I and OE to decrease? Discuss with each other how to change these simple indicators. I would like to see your performance evaluations include how many times you've moved one of the measurements in the desired direction."

The professor started to rub his balding head. "What is the goal of this company?"

"To grow people and make money," said Ashley.

"Beautiful," declared Keen. "How much job security do we have if Magic doesn't make money?"

"None," was the reply.

"I'm glad we're having these learning sessions," Chris admitted suddenly. "I never thought I'd get paid for sitting in classes and learning."

"Your responsibility, Chris, is now to use it for the betterment of Magic and yourself," the professor pointed out. "That is how you really express how well you have learned and appreciate these opportunities that Peter is giving us. Since there don't seem to be any more questions, go forth and put into practice the ideas we just shared. Thanks for coming."

20

Suggestion System

"What Have You Learned and Implemented from Benchmarking This Month?"

While Peter was on one of his many trips, he read that problem solving was not well applied in many organizations. He was more and more concerned about frustrating Magic's employees by not having a standardized system that would enable them to solve technical and process problems. Peter recalled several conversations that he and Keen had had on trying to locate a technique or method to address this issue. Peter decided to telephone John.

"Good morning, John."

"Peter! How was your trip?"

"Great. I learned a lot. I always come back excited about what we can do but at the same time depressed about how far we have to go to be competitive."

"Peter, Rome wasn't built in a day. Haven't you always done this after each trip?"

"Most trips, yes."

"It seems to me that you can't measure the success and fruitfulness of your trips by your up and down barometer of excitement and depression. One thing I have learned from you is that after every visit to another firm you and Magic's employees return and implement some world-class idea that you've seen. Peter, would you believe that a couple of other firms (thanks to your compliments about me that I am now working with) don't even think of doing this. I have started to ask them at every monthly meeting *'what have you learned and implemented from your benchmarking this month?'* They are finally starting to be more sensitive to receiving a return on their time spent learning from different companies."

"I agree, John. The reason I called you was to establish a time this week that we can dialogue on problem solving techniques that we should use at Magic."

"Let me pull my schedule book out. Will tomorrow morning at Zeke's greasy spoon work for you?"

"See you there."

As usual, both Peter and John were a few minutes early. After they ordered some food and coffee they started discussing problem solving.

"The last time we visited problem solving we shared about brainstorming, fishbone diagrams and suggestion systems," said Keen. "My bias is that a suggestion system is a quality of life issue."

"I feel the same way. During one of my visits to another company in my continuous improvement user's group (CIUG). I noticed a storyboard posted on a board that was addressing a problem. In fact, I brought a letter size picture of it back. Here, take a look at it."

"Peter, did you notice that they have tied this back to Dr. Deming's Plan, Do, Check, Act Cycle (P.D.C.A.)?"

"Yes I knew that would turn you on. It shows the eight steps of the storyboard in a clear fashion. Did you notice that the master copy given me includes other suggested statistical tools, too?"

"This is great," said Keen. "Can we get any literature or read more about it?"

"I already have some literature. Florida Power and Light received the Deming Award and someone from their Deming Team wrote an article on how it works. Here is your copy."

"Thanks."

Peter said, "I'm going to call the utility company and try to locate the author to see if he will come and educate us."

"I always look forward to new things," said Keen. "Thanks."

"Pass the syrup, please."

"All the running and tennis playing that you do allows you to eat this sweet stuff without gaining weight?"

"John, I've never had to fight the waist line battle. I don't sit or stand still very long."

"I've noticed. Let's take a few minutes and discuss this suggestion system. What's your opinion about it?"

"I really don't think much of suggestion systems that have people put their ideas in a box and they don't have to sign them. First of all, they aren't practicing TRIC. Secondly, more times than not, the suggestion isn't completely clear and you would like to ask for more information and details and don't know who to contact."

"What is your idea of a good system?"

"First, *the idea has to be implemented and operationalized before it counts as a suggestion.* Secondly, I believe every person working at Magic should be given a goal of at least five implemented world-class ideas each year."

"I never thought of it that way," Keen commented. "However, the thought of each person at a company coming up with ideas each year is valid and good. Would you tie their annual performance measurement into how many implemented world-class ideas they have each year?"

"I haven't thought about that angle. However, I do like the idea."

"What are your thoughts on rewarding people for implementing world-class ideas?" asked Keen.

"I know one argument says you pay them to work and to improve their jobs. You shouldn't pay them for what they are supposed to do in the first place. However, I believe some nominal and monetary reward for recognition would be beneficial."

"Okay Peter, you've thought this through . . . so let's hear it."

"I am going to post an expectation on the information boards that our goal is to achieve 500 implemented world-class ideas this year. It'll be just like our old safety number system. We'll change the number every week to see how many we've achieved to date."

"Do you plan to have each person achieve a minimum number each year?"

"No. I just want to introduce the concept and see what happens the first year. Some time down the road we'll probably tie it somehow into individual expectations."

"What kind of recognition reward are you thinking about at this time?"

"I plan after 15 suggestions to place them all in a hat or box and have someone draw a winner. The winner will receive a $50 gift certificate to Wal-Mart. The purpose of choosing one at random is so as not to distinguish between the perceived size or magnitude of the suggestion. Maybe one idea saves us $5 and another saves us $1,000. We need them all. I want everyone to think and act Kaizen all the time in every way. Every suggestion has an equal chance of winning."

"Keen, that's terrific. Do you feel that everyone understands the concept?"

"I do."

"Will the reward be the same if more than one person shares the suggestion?"

"Every idea drawn as the winner receives $50 and how they want to split it is up to the associates. I've got to believe that they'll split it evenly amongst themselves."

"Any thought about the tribal history aspect?"

John, you know me. I never leave home without my camera."

"Can you cover all the stories though? Shouldn't you have some kind of an expectation for recording these ideas?"

"What did you have in mind?" Peter asked as he put a fork full of pancakes into his mouth.

"The professor envied his friend's metabolism. "Pass the coffee, please," Keen asked. Peter pored himself a cup and then passed the pot to Keen. "Thank you, Peter."

After pouring his coffee, Keen began. "Peter, I've learned this from you. Take a picture of the idea before and after it is implemented. Post the pictures by the cafeteria where everyone passes a few times a day. They'll get the idea that others are achieving world-class ideas and they should, too. More so though, I would like to think that someone by observing somebody else's idea might be able to adapt it somehow to their own area of responsibility. Something like an idea board for other ideas. It's Magic's version of the forthcoming 'information highway.'"

"John, I like those ideas. I'll discuss them with the leads and see what they have to say."

"What do you think about flexible worker skills?"

"I believe that they are the way of the future. Why do you ask?"

"It is my belief that a worker grows faster and is more valuable to a company if management has a skills chart or a path for an individual to follow. Really, it is another one of those quality of life issues in my way of thinking."

"Are you suggesting that Magic do something formal along these lines?"

"Just an idea for another day."

"How many of those quality of life issues have you hung your hat on to date? Let me try to identify them. Housekeeping, safety, preventive maintenance, celebrations, problem solving, suggestion system, and now flexible skill charting. Any more?"

"Maybe. But you have identified all of them for now. Peter, I truly believe that by Magic's addressing these issues early on that the workers appreciate it, more readily accept change, and because of the constant change grow as individuals."

"We've already seen this," Peter pointed out. "People are caring more for each other and are looking for ways to help each other. They are suggesting more and more things for us to consider. Housekeeping, safety, preventive maintenance have improved many fold since we first started sharing our similar and different management philosophies."

"What do you mean ... different philosophies?" Keen asked. "You've just had the wrong slant on some things."

"Right. I guess you want me to buy into your philosophy of my picking up the breakfast tab this morning?"

"I can accept your philosophy," said Keen.

21

Business Philosophy

"Change Should Be Gradual and
Constant, Rather Than Abrupt and Volatile"

Keen was walking around the factory floor, chitchatting with people in each department. He liked to make inquiries that helped him to gain a clearer understanding of everything and to solicit opinions about things that were happening or were just about to happen at the company. This morning he was interested in the workers' opinions on worker skills.

During his conversation with Mark in the pressroom, Keen asked Mark what he thought of having a plan for each employee to improve his or her work skills. Mark liked the idea as long as there was adequate training and coaching, along with some financial reward.

"What's your idea of a financial reward?" asked Keen.

"I don't have anything in particular in mind, but it's along the lines you discussed in one of your meetings. You said that the more documented skills one had, the more valuable he or she was to an organization and that this person should receive more pay."

Keen added, "I also believe that a person should be able not only to do everything required at a workstation, but also to do preventive and predictive maintenance and minor repairs. Another stipulation is that he or she be certified as having those skills not only by someone within his or her work cell, but also by someone independent of the work cell. Plus I believe that there should be at least a one-year period before someone can move to a higher certified skill level."

Mark was slightly taken aback by the professor's comments. "John, isn't that a long waiting period?"

"I don't think so. There are many different jobs done at one work cell and different problems appear at different times. I just feel that by going through one complete twelve-month period, a person probably faces every situation that happens there. This also provides the person sufficient time to become so proficient that there is little chance of the person not measuring up to the certification process."

"Oh, I understand what you mean," said Mark. "You're trying to assure that the worker has a high chance of being successful."

"That is certainly true. I also would like to see that everyone write in their yearly goal statement a skill level that they aspire to for the next twelve months." Keen was not averse to doing this in a shorter length of time, but to allow a year just seemed to be a more sound practice in terms of building the experience and expectations of the worker.

The professor also knew that as Magic became more and more automated, the flexible worker concept had to become a reality. Workers needed to know how to do more things. It was simply a matter of time before Magic caught the wind of change toward greater automation.

Keen continued his excursion through the plant. As he strolled past the assembly department, he saw Peter on the factory floor, talking to the assembly workers about various issues. Keen stopped to listen.

Peter was explaining to the group that Magic had to become more visual in its communication of what was expected and happening at the company. He referred to the way some companies used key performance indicator boards (KPIs) with broad measurements related to Quality, Costs, Delivery, Safety, and Morale (Q, C, D, S, M), something he had learned from Kio Suzaki, an author and guest speaker. Under each one of the five broad measurements were more detailed measures developed by the work area to help continuous improvement take place. He was investigating how Magic might go about adopting this concept. As soon as he learned more about it he would share it in more detail with them. In the meantime he wanted them to think about it.

After Peter finished talking to the group, he spotted Keen and walked over. "You should be very proud of them from what I can tell," said Keen.

"I am. This place is definitely better organized. More things have seemed to find homes and are there until they're needed."

Keen smiled, because he knew about Peter's fetish with housekeeping and organization. "I hear that more of your customers and suppliers have been complimenting you about the cleanliness and orderliness of the plant."

"That's right. And housekeeping isn't our only improvement. Fred has kept maintenance busy. The workers are pleased that the machines and tools are now more reliable. We've taken care of every safety item that the workers have called to our attention. I really feel good about all of this."

"You should, Peter. We have talked often about the quality of life issues that should be addressed early on when trying to change a culture. The more the workers feel that you have their best interests at heart, the more they are willing to cooperate and get involved with what is happening. You have done a nice job in helping people grow."

"John, don't forget that you've been a part of it too."

Keen stopped to think about this chance combination of academic theory and everyday business. What a long way he and Peter had come. It *was* working. Magic had grappled with enormously complicated changes in its operation and its culture. The results were evident.

Peter thought of all the busy summers (as well as autumns, winters, and springs) he had had during the past few years, the countless meetings and workshops. And he also thought of all the changes that had taken place, in both his personal and his business life. "You know, Professor Keen," Peter said jokingly, "at fifty years old, I have changed my business philosophy in many areas."

"No-o-o," the professor teased. He knew that Peter had changed his views. After all, he had been with him through a lot of the transformation. But he was curious to hear Peter put it all into perspective. So, as usual, he asked Peter a question. "In what way?"

"Well, I can think of several things off the top of my head. The importance of the people, good leadership, competition, and what it takes to succeed."

Keen found this quite interesting. "Would you care to elaborate on the changes during your business career?"

"You know some of them because you've been with me during most of their implementation. First of all, I now know the true value of the power of the people and good leadership."

Throughout his business career, Peter had never taken workers for granted. But he was now even more convinced of their importance and intrinsic worth. If it were not for the people and good leadership, very few of the changes at Magic could have taken place. He had worked for bosses who had provided little support or leadership.

"I've also come to understand that you run a going concern differently from one with a cash flow problem or one that's on the verge of Chapter 11."

"How is that?" Keen asked, "and why?"

"Primarily because the company on the verge of bankruptcy needs a benevolent dictator—they cannot afford mistakes and they have to move fast. A going concern has the time to educate and train the associates—including the managers—about the tools of an empowered workforce. They also have the time to develop a vision for the company and a road map for everyone to follow to the vision. The stronger companies are the ones where the top person is able to clearly communicate where the organization is headed and has a mission statement for how to accomplish the vision. I've learned that it takes time to disseminate the vision and an even longer period of time for the people to internalize its meaning."

"Interesting," Keen thought to himself. "Another experiential aha."

"Getting this buy-in takes good leadership. It takes leaders who set the example and live it with a passion. And I don't mean leaders who say 'we want to be the best' and then leave everyone hanging without the road map or tools to accomplish being the best. You and I both know these leaders. If you want cleanliness, then you must live it and show what it means. I could go on for hours, but I think you understand."

"I do. I do. It sounds like what you did in the beginning—mopping the floors, cleaning the restrooms, wiping down the machines."

The two men paused to reflect on the metamorphosis that had taken place. Keen then asked, "How have you changed your views toward competition?"

"I used to think they were the enemy. Being born in the 1940s, and raised and educated in the 1950s and 1960s—competition was the enemy. You did not share ideas with your competition, and in many cases you did not even talk to them. I now ask myself, how do you know if you are good at what you do? How can you really improve? And what pushes you to succeed? If you never meet or visit someone in the same business, how can you rate your own performance?"

Peter stopped to emphasize the questions he had raised. "*The change in our culture has made Magic successful.* We can't deny that technology is important, but you have to have associates who understand what is going on in the world. There has to be a global perspective. People say that the world has shrunk. Well, it has, and our customers today buy products from all around the world. Of course, it's because of the better communications and transportation that we have today. But today's customer wants quality, cost, and delivery. And they will buy from whoever can provide it."

Keen and Peter had talked extensively about the global marketplace, and about the fact that competitors and customers are no longer in the same city, state, or even country. They can be anywhere in the world.

"If we're going to keep our customers, we have to know what is going on in the world market—that includes technology, processes, management, and people programs," Peter explained. "Networking or benchmarking is one way to find out how well you are doing and how much you have to improve. You cannot live in a vacuum. If you live in a vacuum, you will never grow. You have to network with many companies to grow and learn and improve. This includes benchmarking your competition. Of course, this is hard because many people do not understand that they need a paradigm shift."

Keen was immensely impressed with his friend's wisdom. "What would you say has been your most significant insight?"

"I think the biggest lesson in my lifetime has been Kaizen—small steps of continuous improvement."

Peter could tell from the professor's expression that he needed to elaborate. "You need to take small steps of incremental improvement instead of large steps. *Change should be gradual and constant, rather than abrupt and volatile.* The overall effect should be long-term, long-lasting, and undramatic, instead of short-term and dramatic. Take the typical suggestion system, for example. It does not encourage involvement or teamwork. By paying a percentage of potential savings to a small group of people, most associates are excluded. Everyone's looking for the big bucks.

"Last month I was invited to speak to a local Rotary Club about Magic and our changes. The junior Rotarian who spoke before me had been accepted by one of the leading engineering schools in the country. He told us that after graduation from college, he was going to start a business, run it for four or five years, then sell the business and retire in style. He has the 'get rich quick syndrome,' or, as I call it, the 'lotto mentality.' We need to tell everyone, especially young people, that lasting improvement comes in small doses. What good is it to win the battle and lose the war?"

Keen saw the light. "Small steps for long-lasting results."

"That's right. We have to stop looking for $1,000 bills and start taking care of the dollars. Most of us, though, think that we'll get overnight results. We don't realize that it takes years. In fact, this principle has taken me several years to learn—without even realizing I was learning it.

"When we first started making changes at Magic we were following many of the Kaizen concepts without realizing it. First, management has to change, and that can take years. Next, middle management has to learn and buy in, which could take longer than it takes management. Finally, you start the training of all your associates for continuous improvement in small, incremental steps. But, as we have found out and as Kaizen states, the true answer is to *get people involved.*"

22

Rearview Management

"None of Us Is as Smart as All of Us" Roy Disney

The summer had flown by, and nature's magnificent colors were notice- able everywhere as Keen drove to meet Chet, Peter, and Fred for their monthly "everything dialogue" meeting at Zeke's greasy spoon. He was admiring the beauty of the season change and daydreaming about how nice things were in general.

During the short drive to the diner, Keen thought of how too many com- panies manage by looking in their rearview mirrors while trying to com- pete in a forward-looking world. They always seem to be fighting fires. They also do not have a strong management commitment to making the necessary changes for the future.

Keen reflected on the questions he often asked management groups that he spoke to. One of the first questions was *"What do you spend most of your time on at work every day?"* Almost 100 percent of the time the immediate answer was "fighting fires." He would then ask them how much of their daily time was used for fighting fires. Invariably the response was, "between 50 and 90 percent." Finally, he would ask them what they did with the balance of their time. There were all kinds of answers. After all of the answers were volunteered, Keen would offer his own explanation: "You start fires. This is called job security." His answer always brought loud laughter.

Keen told managers that by adopting this fire-fighting mentality, they were really driving their company by looking in the rearview mirror. "You don't take time to fix the problems causing the fires," he would tell them. "So you're always looking back to see what damage control you can employ to survive today's crashes."

As he drove into the diner's parking lot, Keen could not wait to hear what the team had to say about why setup time reduction was in a stall. As he walked to the table, Peter was the first one to greet him. "Good morning, professor. We've already been talking about the usual personnel situations and our delivery challenges. I wanted to wait until you got here to discuss setup time reduction."

Keen was glad. "I have not heard about or seen much action regarding setup time reduction. This bothers me because it is the +1 in the 4+1 focus program we have. Why hasn't there been much action?"

Fred spoke up. "It's my fault. I was assigned the responsibility to lead that focus group and we haven't done that much. I've been so busy attending other meetings that I put setup time reduction on the back burner."

"What does the +1 mean to all the people at Magic?" asked Peter.

"I know it's our primary focus for strengthening a weak link," responded Fred. "But I need help."

"What would you think if we built the idea around the 'Indy 500' auto race?" asked Keen. "When one of those precision cars pulls into the pit, how long does it take the pit crew to get the car back into the race?"

All three said, "Seconds."

"Right. That's the image we want everyone at Magic to have. Our presses and dies are our precision engines that drive Magic's sales. Since we are a job order shop, when the machines aren't running the throughput at Magic is zero. You could say the heartbeat of Magic has stopped. What do we do when someone's heart stops beating?"

"Mouth-to-mouth resuscitation," said Chet, who had been a medic in the armed services before he joined Magic.

"Correct," said Keen. "So when one of our machines has to come into the pit area for a die changeover, we want a highly synchronous, trained pit crew to climb all over that machine and get it back in the race in the shortest time possible. We want the sales meter running—or breathing—all the time, because that's how we make money."

"I like the pit crew motif, but how are we going to train these people?" asked Fred. "This has been my problem up to now."

"Give them a chance," challenged Peter. "Look at all the different solutions they've come up with for the other focus groups we've established. Things that none of us would have thought of for the rest of our lives. They're doing this because we're using their brains as well as their brawn."

"Do you know what Roy Disney said?" Keen asked.

"*If you can dream it, you can do it*," said Chet.

"That was Walt Disney who said that," Peter remarked, "and I do believe it."

"So do I," Keen said. "Roy was alleged to have said '*None of us is as smart as all of us.*'"

"I've got a suggestion," said Peter. "We can send some of our key people off to seminars, purchase some materials to read, bring in a reputable consultant on quick exchange of dies, network with other companies that are working on this issue, and ask around town for ideas."

Keen jumped back into the dialogue, "What about rally days? The purpose of a rally for Magic's Pit Crew teams would be to educate, share information, praise them for accomplishments, and encourage them to keep fired up about reaching our improvement goals. Fred, what do you think of approaching the focus team with this idea?" asked Keen.

"I'm a gamer," said Fred. "I like it and believe it'll work. Are you planning to attend the meetings?"

"I wouldn't miss the big race for anything," declared Keen. "I will be there."

23

Robust Process

"Pay Me Now, or Pay Me Later"

Communication—along with almost everything else at Magic—was improving. Management was being more honest with the workers as well as with themselves. Weaknesses and shortcomings were seen as parts of life, not something to hide. Most of Magic's associates recognized and appreciated the positive changes taking place. There was a feeling of esprit de corps and the unspoken but palpable unity of a true team.

The professor thought about how he and Chet had been working weekly with the focus groups to reduce setup time for the press and the four-slide machines. Both the pressroom and the four-slide area were mini-companies—cross-functional, self-directed work teams with their own "company officers," vision and mission statements, business plans, and key performance indicators. Peter and Fred generally were aware of the progress there but did not know all the details. Maybe if they did, they could add ways to make things even better. Keen was also wondering why Magic had not involved suppliers and customers more in the designing of new parts. He would bring that up, too.

"Good morning," Keen said, as he arrived at Zeke's Restaurant.

"Good morning," Fred answered, looking up from a cup of coffee.

A few minutes later Peter and Chet arrived, right on time, and all four men ordered breakfast.

As usual, their meeting started out with personnel issues. After a while, Keen said that he and Chet would like to share more in-depth information about what was happening with the Pit Crew teams. They wanted to bring Peter and Fred up to date on the details and get their feedback. "John and I have been meeting once a week for an hour on Thursdays with the Pressroom Pit Crew and a Four-Slide Pit Crew Team," Chet began. "Each team has a lead, a tool maker who works on their tools, the lead of the toolroom, an operator, and one person who works the second shift. We've held a few rally days and have sent some of the crew members to association meetings and to other companies to learn new ways of how to improve our operations. We've had a well-known setup reduction consultant in to spend a day teaching and trouble shooting all the machines in the pressroom and four-slide area, and we've even had outside toolmakers in for a working lunch to introduce them to what we're doing about standardizing our tools."

"How did the meeting go with the outside toolmakers we use?" asked Peter.

"They were impressed with what we're doing. We had a good exchange of ideas, and they understand Magic's expectations of them regarding all the future tooling being built for us. I believe everyone gained from the experience."

Keen agreed with Chet.

"You were there too?" Peter asked.

"Yes, I was," Keen replied. "I learned a lot from everyone."

"John is never lost for questions and clarification statements," Chet joked. "He asked some questions that we assumed were clear to everyone, but John somehow asked them in that innocent way of his that we find challenging and useful. We discovered for ourselves that there were several viewpoints about the best way to do something or other when we started answering his questions. This led to all of us learning something more.

"Every week we have been graphing and posting our progress," Chet continued. "Once we crossed the 50 percent mark for standardizing the tools, we held a celebration rally and shared what had been done and what we expected to accomplish in the future. We also asked everyone for his or her ideas on what else could be done to enhance the process of reducing setup times. At every rally we receive more good ideas about how to improve, and we incorporate them into the process as soon as we can. People are really buying into this because they see progress and their jobs are getting easier to set up."

Chet took a sip of coffee and the professor jumped in. "We've eliminated waste and worker frustration at the same time," he said. "People want to do the right things, and we have to continue to improve the system for them. This is fun, and we are all growing in confidence, appreciation, and the willingness to take more risks."

"I'm impressed," said Peter. "Would you do me a favor? Put a copy of your weekly agenda and minutes in my mailbox, so that I can keep up with the pit crew. I know they're in the fast lane, but—at least as a spectator—I want to enjoy Magic's progress in the race."

"I have a question," said Keen. "Do you know about the shadow influence, where 5 percent of the total costs under traditional accounting measurements drives 80 percent of the ultimate costs of an automobile?" asked Keen.

"Yes," said both Peter and Fred.

"What are we going to do about it at Magic?"

Everyone knew that Keen was setting him or her up for something.

On cue, Peter asked, "What do you have in mind, John?"

"A robust process that coordinates and synchronizes everyone from design concept to production run," stated Keen. "I believe that we should identify all the steps that Magic has to take in order to make the part production ready. It's like the idea from the ad, '*Pay me now, or pay me later.*' It will take us longer to design each part and to prototype it before production, but once production starts, the workers will not have nearly as many problems trying to make the parts correctly. By having the input from everyone outside and inside Magic involved on the front end of production process, our quality costs will be lower, on-time delivery will be easier to achieve, lead times will be shorter, engineering changes will be minimal, and we'll have a satisfied customer every time."

Keen explained that after this "robust process" was completed, everyone involved would have bought into the rationale behind a certain part and would understand why changes had to be made. He pointed out that knowledge and understanding reduce or eliminates workers' frustrations over short setup times and increase their willingness to turn out quality parts. The engineers, quality people, and toolmakers, by seeing their efforts result in customers' and workers' satisfaction, would feel good about themselves and contribute to the quality of life at Magic.

"This will help create a work environment where people have fun and share ideas," Keen declared, "and where more people will continuously make positive contributions to the overall welfare."

"Schedule a time and we'll get started," said Peter.

The process never ends. The combination of good ideas and documented implementation never ceases to improve the world at Magic. The company was getting used to a life of continuous improvement through continuous questioning and continuous learning.

24

It's Not Magic—Continuous Education

"In the Future It Won't Matter Whether or Not You Have a Diploma or Degree"

Magic's hard work in growing people was indeed paying off. Pit crews, rallies, focus groups, growing people—the change in the language at Magic was proof.

Keen thought, "why can't every other company emulate this?" But he knew the answer: It goes back to leadership and the people and their willingness to change. It's not magic but simply learning how to grow people.

It was the dead of winter and the roads were slick. As Keen drove around the frozen lake to get on the highway to Magic, he was hoping that he would be able to spend some time with Peter discussing educational concerns. Peter had always had insights and angles on the issues that Keen did not.

When Keen arrived at the plant, he walked through the office area on his way to the engineering conference room. He still had a few minutes before the pit crew meeting started, so he poked his head into Peter's office. "How are you doing today?" the professor asked.

"Fine," Peter said, looking up from his desk. "What are you here for today?"

"I have a pit crew meeting in a few minutes."

"How's that going?"

"The pressroom is doing great!"

"Yes, I heard that, and I am pleased at the progress they have made. What are you doing after the meeting?"

"I was going to go back to the university to work."

"Come see me in a little while, after you finish the pit crew meeting. Maybe we can talk about some educational issues for a few minutes. Do you have time to do it?" Ah, thought Keen, if only all my clients were that much in sync with me.

After Keen finished the pit crew meeting, he headed straight to Peter's office. "Well, we both feel strongly about education," Peter said. "And everyone should realize that education and training must be an ongoing program for any company that hopes to be world-class. After all, nothing is more essential to the successful implementation of world-class manufacturing and to maintaining the competitive edge advantage than continuous education."

"I couldn't agree with you more," Keen said. "Perhaps the biggest single misconception about education that is the idea that education and training is a one-shot effort. At least 50 percent of what an engineer, lawyer, doctor, or educator learns is obsolete in three to six years. In the future we are told that the cycle will be more like one or two years.

"All the new software on how to access library materials from anywhere at anytime and the hundreds of educational software packages available to teachers are mind-boggling. It's difficult just to keep up with what is available, much less learn how to skillfully use it."

"That's also true in manufacturing," Peter pointed out. "Magic is continuously bombarded with new software for the office and the factory floor. The one thing that I insist on is that our engineers and toolroom personnel have the latest software available for design, engineering, and tool building. Our customers are a big help to us in this area. Our project engineers are in daily contact with most of them, and we usually visit each other about once a week to keep abreast of all the existing and future jobs. We have built good working partnerships with most of our major customers. They share with us what they have learned about the new software available and what they think about the software that they have acquired."

The professor added, "The new technology of learning will enable virtually every learner to master every module of every course and of every subject. Why not? Isn't that what we should want to do for everyone?"

"In the future it won't matter whether or not you have a diploma or degree," Peter said. "*One's future will be based on reliable instruments that certify attainment of competency regardless of where or how you learned it.*"

Chet looked in and interrupted the discussion. "Pardon me, but we have a problem with parts for Zephyr Stamping Company."

"What is it?" Peter asked.

"Our inventory records show that we have enough finished goods and steel to supply them what they want. They normally take 100,000 parts a week but they just called and they want 500,000 in two weeks. As you know, car sales are terrific."

"What's the problem?" Peter asked.

"We don't have the steel to make the number of parts that they want," Chet explained. "Somebody made an engineering change and wanted some sample parts for testing. So our pressroom used some of the raw stock for this purpose, and no one entered the inventory reduction into our records. Also, one of the new hires on the second shift used a few coils of steel, got busy, and forgot to relieve the inventory of the amount used. We have called our steel supplier and they can't get us any steel until two weeks from now because of the strong demand for cars—and because of the strike at one of the large steel mills that they use."

"What's your game plan?" asked Peter.

"I'm not sure at this time but I wanted you to know."

"Let's have the steel service center put an inquiry out on their network system," Peter suggested. "Give me a few minutes and I'll get with you. We're wrapping things up here now."

Chet said good-bye and headed back to the shop floor.

Peter said to Keen, "That's what I mean by competence—knowledge joined to passion and commitment. That's what I see more and more of at Magic every day."

Keen turned to go. "Chet's not the only one learning here. The job now is to keep learning—there will always be something new to learn."

25

Reflections

"It's Never Ending Journey"

Another company-wide rally was about to take place at Magic. The sky was clear and the sun was shining. The long winter had turned into a beautiful spring. The event was to be held outside in Magic's large courtyard, the brainchild of several employees. Two years ago, a few of the workers were upset about not being able to eat their lunches outside during ten straight days of rain. They met with Peter and offered to put up an awning behind the plant—at their own expense. But Peter liked their idea so much that he immediately began to brainstorm with them, and the courtyard was born.

Peter placed the four workers in charge of the project, and they began sketching blueprints and taking measurements. They presented the information to Peter. Without any delay, he allocated the funds to purchase all of the necessary building materials. The materials were delivered by the end of that week, and they decided to hold a pavilion-building party that Saturday. To everyone's surprise, over one hundred people—including Peter, Keen, Magic's workers, most of the leads, and numerous family members—showed up to build the pavilion and a dozen picnic tables. The group used an existing paved area connected to the back of the plant as the courtyard's patio, and they built a large shelter above the patio.

The pavilion and picnic tables gave the area a park-like atmosphere. To the right of the courtyard was the parking lot, but employees planted evergreens along the fence to make the view more pleasant. To the left of the courtyard were a stream and a thick row of bushes and trees. Behind Magic was a large field of wildflowers.

The courtyard was a good investment. It built a family atmosphere and continues to boost morale. Workers used it practically every day for their lunch breaks, and it was frequently used for meetings, pizza parties, and rallies.

As it is being used today.

Peter opened the rally by unveiling the newest collage. It was the 22nd he had done, and it contained nearly 350 pictures. In the center of the collage was a brief list of accomplishments that had taken place at Magic since the last collage a few months ago.

After Peter's presentation, Chet and Ashley gave out several awards and gift certificates. Following the awards, a member from each focus group stood up and spotlighted the achievements of the group and the goals that had been set.

Besides celebrating various achievements, today also marked five years since Peter had purchased the company. The people at Magic wanted to thank him for everything he had done. They stood up and sang "For He's a Jolly Good Fellow" as Peter's wife and children came out of the building. Emotions were running high. Many of the workers and leads had cards for Peter. It was a touching moment for everyone, especially Peter.

But the highlight of the rally was a welcome-back celebration for Walter and Doug from the spring mini-company. The two men had just returned from an eight-day trip to Japan—paid for by Magic. They attended several conferences and an international trade show, where they examined the latest manufacturing equipment and other technology. In addition, they were invited to visit two of the country's premier manufacturing companies.

Fred stood up and announced Walter and Doug. Everyone began clapping and whistling. But the applause soon quieted down because the two voyagers had disappeared. They had been sitting together in the rear of the courtyard, and now they were gone.

All of a sudden, Japanese music could be heard over the loudspeakers. Then a low resonant bong rang out from a tam-tam. As if by magic, the door of the plant opened, and out stepped Walter and Doug dressed in kimonos.

A roar erupted from the crowd. The long robes and broad sashes were a hit with the group, partly because of the beauty of the garments, but also because the demonstration was so unexpected. Walter is an older, large, rough-looking man. Doug is slight and somewhat shy. The two of them in brightly colored kimonos was a sight to behold. And when they began modeling their attire with a few turns and twists and exaggerated movements, everyone burst into laughter.

After the laughter died down, Walter and Doug spent about twenty minutes sharing their experiences from the trip. They would go into more detail about their findings at next month's life-long education meeting. They also planned on talking about Japan's culture.

As was customary, the entire event was being videotaped from the back of the room. The tape would be added to the growing library of audio and visual cassettes to keep a record of the small pieces of tribal history. Guests occasionally attended Magic's celebrations. Today, there were quite a few family members and visitors due to Peter's fifth anniversary celebration.

There was also a reporter from one of the trade publications in attendance. During the past few years this journalist had written several articles about Magic and various aspects of the company, ranging from its quality program to the improved communication. The event took him by surprise. Even though he had attended other companies' rallies, this one was different. He instantly felt like one of the family, and got so wrapped up in the celebrating that he almost forgot to take notes and snap photos. This was one writing assignment he was glad he had accepted.

After the rally, he interviewed several of the workers, who were only too glad to boast about *their* company and *their* associates. The workers spoke about their fellow associates, culture, communication, and trust in words not usually associated with a manufacturing plant.

Keen had to leave immediately after the rally to meet with a potential client. He did not get to be interviewed by the reporter, or have any dessert, or talk with Peter. Three things that he loved. But he was pleased with the rally. He always left Magic's celebrations feeling rejuvenated. Keen was proud. He was content. And he was happy.

His consulting opportunities had expanded thanks to Peter's recommendations. Keen was trying to teach other organizations how to change culture and grow people. Keen just hoped that other companies could improve as much as Magic. He quickly learned that every company is unique in its leadership and commitment. Every company approached the same concepts with different ideas of how to implement them and with varying degrees of commitment. If the management was not willing to put forth the necessary time and effort to make appropriate changes, they would never improve their culture or grow people. At Peter's suggestion, Keen had resigned from a few companies because top management did not walk the talk or have the full commitment or patience to bring about the needed change.

147

As the courtyard cleared out and the parking lot emptied, Peter took a quiet walk through the field behind the factory with his six-year-old granddaughter. It had been a long week. Peter had had several meetings, a couple fires to put out, and twice he had had to stay quite late. The rally was a great way to end a tiring week. But Peter's week was not exactly over. Tomorrow he would be flying to a manufacturing conference where he was a keynote speaker.

Peter enjoyed these speaking engagements. They gave him a chance to share his experiences with others. Doing so provided him with a sense of accomplishment, a sense of pride, pride in himself and in everyone associated with Magic. The speeches were easy for him. He simply talked about Magic's successes and concepts. He talked about what he and the leads and the associates had done, and how and why they had done it. The audience could always tell he was speaking from his heart.

While walking and watching his granddaughter run through the tall grass, Peter reflected on Magic and the way it was when he had bought the company five years ago.

No quality systems
No quality manuals
No statistical process control
No engineers
No tracking of anything
No numerically controlled machines
No computers
No training

Peter thought back to when Magic started to track on-time deliveries. They were at 60 percent. He also thought about his first visit a few years ago with Mr. Moore at Acme, Magic's largest customer. Mr. Moore had told him that Magic could not even handle the business Acme gave them then. How could they possibly handle any more?

Today, Magic chooses not to do business with Acme at all. In the quest to improve, Magic realized that having a smaller customer base and serving them well was a much more productive strategy than taking all comers. He also reminisced about the biggest hurdle during the first year—when the single largest product (over 60 percent of the overall business) was being obsoleted. Yes, today, Magic is a different company.

> Strong quality systems and a good quality manual
> Token Ring Network connecting all of the company's computer systems
> Operators do SPC with electronic gauges into a computer system. They have access to CAD files, visual aids, inspection requirements, and past history
> 50 PCs for their 100 employees; Finite Element Analysis and CAD/CAM capabilities
> Twelve engineers, plus six Certified Quality Engineers (CQEs)
> On-time delivery averaging 98.5 percent
> Cost of quality at less than 2 percent
> CPK average of 1.75
> Twelve implemented ideas per employee per year
> Improved parts per million (PPM) to single digit in several minicompanies
> A reduction of inventory by 30 percent, even though sales have tripled

Today the company is a showplace. Many of the associates say the plant is cleaner than their homes. Peter thought to himself, the most important measurement is how our associates have grown. Five years ago Magic was lacking a lot, but it did have good associates who were willing to learn. In fact, in most cases they accepted new ideas and change faster than anyone thought possible.

Peter glanced over at his granddaughter chasing a butterfly. Her small arms were outstretched overhead in an attempt to catch the colorful insect, which was well beyond reach. Peter stopped to watch her and wait for her to return. After a few minutes, he began to think again about the people at Magic and what a long way everyone had come during the last four years in making professional, personal, and social changes.

> No on-floor inspectors; each operator does his or her own inspections
> No time clocks
> Flex-hours
> Decision-making and problem-solving done on the plant floor
> Company celebrations monthly
> Life-long education program
> Many companies visit for benchmarking purposes
> No barriers between office/plant; no walls—period
> Visual communications—charts and graphs everywhere
> Meetings and educational systems used to communicate.

Peter looked across the field. "Today is a great day," he declared to himself. "And the future looks bright." He imagined what still lay ahead. "We still need to improve the robust process; more teaching is needed about discipline and how to constructively handle criticism; additional development of the Smart Tools is required; continuation of the quality of life issues; striving for the lean production principles; more employee education programs are needed; and, in fact, just holding the gains that we have achieved and continuously looking forward for more betterment is a challenge. It is overwhelming at times but—by the inch it's a cinch, by the yard it's hard.

"We have all the tools in place, and a positive culture that accepts change. Now all we need is continued leadership to follow that road towards customer satisfaction based on a quality focus. *It is a never-ending journey.*"

Peter thought about how quickly things had changed at Magic after they were able to open up the spirit of communication. They were able to draw upon a wealth of talent. And he saw the spirit of everyone in the organization improve.

"Yes," Peter thought to himself as he turned to head back to the plant, "It's easy to talk about Magic and the changes. It's easy to tell people how to do it. It's easy to tell them why to do it. It's easy to get people excited about what they can accomplish. But improving your culture and growing people and making the 1,001 necessary changes isn't easy. It takes a tremendous amount of time, effort and commitment from everyone. It's hard work, not magic."

Peter stopped in the middle of the field and looked around. It was a glorious day. Just then his granddaughter tugged on his shirt sleeve. "Look, grandpa," she said, pointing to a shadow that floated across the ground.

The two of them glanced up and saw a large hawk. It circled overhead, like them, enjoying the day. With a quick movement, it flew off toward the sun.

Peter remembered that a hawk is an Indian sign for good fortune. Peter thought to himself about the many things that had transpired to make Magic Manufacturing successful. It was not "magic" but education, hard work, commitment on everyone's part, passion for doing the right things in the right way, caring for each other, employee involvement, and leadership.

The hawk must certainly have been a sign of my good fortune, thought Peter as he surveyed his surroundings and reached down for his granddaughter's hand.